Gini

You're a true Rock Star in this world cuz you've helped thousands build better futures for themselves.

Count me a fan, & thanks for your help with this project!

Warren

THE FUTURE

A powerful truth from Will Rogers:

> "It ain't what folks don't know
> that gets them into trouble.
> It's what they know
> that just ain't so."

And in this book:

> "For many, the biggest danger in this current recession,
> is that it won't last long enough"

"Success is more about courage then capability"

"Thinking outside the box is fine, but what most need is a little more thinking *inside* the box"

"Winning is *not* about brilliant new ideas"

"*Hold hands and stay together* is still great advice"

"Even if you're on the right track, if you sit still long enough you'll eventually get run over. In business, you'll get commoditized"

"*Everybody hates change* is nonsense"

"If you act like a robot you risk being replaced by one"

"The market shall sit in judgement between the quick and the dead"

"Nobody is going to give you your dream job. You're going to have to build it for yourself"

"Yesterday we kept our customers because they knew us. Tomorrow we'll keep them because we know them"

Dedication

for Parker
who would have loved the idea

The Future

a build-your-own-future manual for Administrative Professionals

Warren Evans

Adibooks
181 Industrial Avenue
Lowell, MA 01852

Adibooks
181 Industrial Avenue
Lowell, MA 01852
Ph: 978-458-2345 Fax: 978-458-3026

Copyright © 2009 by Warren Evans Ideas, Inc.
All rights reserved. This book, or parts thereof, may not be reproduced in any form without permission.

Library of Congress Cataloging-in-Publication Data

Evans, Warren.
The future: a build-your-own future manual for administrative professionals / Warren Evans
p. cm.

ISBN 13: 978-0-9841294-0-9

ISBN 10: 0-9841294-0-5

Printed in the United States of America

Cover design by Steve MacEachern

For More Information About

The Future

1-800-364-3205

www.wevans.com

Table of Contents

Introduction	1
Some Perspective	3
A Whole New World	7
Hollywood Days & Cyber Knights	18
A World of Possibilities	35
Building Your Own Future	47
The Macro Trends	69
Technology Creates Transparency	74
Personality is the Brand	82
Micro-marketing	91
The Next Service Revolution	97
Simplification Gets Hot	105
Community Catalysts Conquer	113
More Trends to Watch	118
"And in Summary . . ."	127

Big Time THANKS!

Lots of people pitched in, above and beyond, to make this book possible. All of them under bizarrely tight time frames, which was my fault.

Kudos and thanks are due to the Bear in Boston at Adibooks, Steve at Quack Communications in Erin, Patti at Down to Earth Marketing, also in Erin, and Susan Fenner and all the great people at IAAP.

An eternal debt of gratitude is acknowledged to Susan and Victoria, without whom it simply would not have happened. Period.

All remaining errors are mine and mine alone, for which I apologize. I hope nonetheless that you find it both interesting and useful.

Warren Evans
Toronto
July 2009

Introduction

This is not a book about the future; at least, not about the *distant* future.

There are two reasons for this:

1. As much as we may be personally interested in what will be happening 20 or 30 years from now, it's of little *practical* use, in terms of what we do tomorrow in our careers and our personal lives, as we make decisions on how best to move forward.

2. The other is, frankly, we're not very good at long distance predictions.

In the 60's a Presidential Commission on the Future worried extensively about how we were going to find meaning and fill our lives with the enormous amount of leisure time the predictions indicated. After all, by the turn of the century we were all supposed to be working a 30-hour work week.

How did that turn out for you?

For most of us, it turned out about as well as the paperless office we were all supposed to be working in by now. And the advent of television did not kill radio, nor did the VCR kill movies. This could become a long list.

This is a book about trends that are happening right now. It's about what organizations, and smart professionals at all levels inside them, are doing to ensure they are an integral part of the future.

Seeing where we are is relatively easy. We only need to look around at what happened yesterday and what happened today. Getting this into a larger context and recognizing some perspective is trickier. To determine what direction we're going, it's very helpful to know from what direction we've come. If we understand from which direction we came, it's a lot easier to figure out which direction we're going.

This book will look at where we are right now, and how we got here. It will examine the trends that are happening right now that will significantly impact the next year, or two, or three – whatever we define as the 'immediate future'.

The overriding purpose of this book is to help you see the 'big picture' of what's happening right now, get it into a context, and then make sense of what's driving it and where it's heading; to better understand the forces buffeting your organization, which your management is dealing with right now; to look at how these things may impact you; to stimulate ideas about how you can best thrive in your current job, or to help you recognize options and alternatives that may be worth exploring for YOU!

Warren Evans
Warren@WEvans.com
1 - 800 - 364 - 3205

Some Perspective

A few years ago, my 16-year-old nephew came to live with me for a while. How this came to be is a longer story than you want to hear, but suffice it to say, he had been spending a disproportionate amount of his time, as so many of us did during our own teenage days, endeavoring to demonstrate the veracity of the old adage that " 'young and stupid' is a redundancy in terminology."

Frankly, I had forgotten what it was like to have a teenager in the house; what it was like to live with someone who could not find his way downtown by himself, but knew all about how the entire universe worked.

One day, we're having the inevitable conversation, as often happens in these circumstances, and he's explaining to me how everything is completely different now; how I don't understand anything at all.

(I don't recall from my own teenage years where I thought adults came from, but I have noticed, in talking with teenagers, that they seem to run on a base assumption that the adult they are talking with is someone who was never actually a teenager himself.)

At any rate, we get to the inevitable piece of this conversation where my nephew starts with, "Everything is completely different now. When people your age were my age, you didn't have cell phones, or laptops, or even computers; you didn't have Wii's or iPods; there was no Internet, and you didn't even have e-mail; you didn't have 200 TV channels, satellite TV, CD's, DVD's or Blu-ray; your cars didn't have antilock brakes or airbags; there was no recycling, no high-efficiency appliances; you couldn't do hip replacements, CAT scans, or MRIs..."

I stopped him, smiled (on the inside), and told him he was right. "When people my age were your age," I said, "we didn't have any of those things, and many more. So, *we* invented *all* of them!"

This was apparently a new thought for him, and he had no further comment. Another 'life lesson discussion' had come to a close.

After he wandered off, I began to think about this rather concise recitation of all the things that had changed during the course of my working lifetime. I began to think about just how radically our world, specifically our world of work, has changed in a relatively short period of time.

This seismic kind of change is not unprecedented.
Every generation that goes through a significant change period believes that never has so much changed so fast, and that things

are changing faster now than at any point in history. This, however, is almost never true.

There was a time when an innovative technology swept the universe. It was a new electronic medium that improved communication and greatly increased the flow of information – so much so that it quickly became a worldwide communication vehicle. It was run by what today would be called super 'techies' and 'geek' types, who had their own buzz words and codes. By using this new communication vehicle, they made friends all over the world.

People met and fell in love via this tool. Stocks skyrocketed; fortunes were made and lost – some several times by the same people. Thousands of small, innovative companies ended up consolidating into a few gigantic ones. Early leaders fell by the wayside. Technical enhancements improved constantly, dramatically, and rapidly while the cost utilization fell by 50%, then by 70%, and then by 90%. Governments and operating companies scrambled to censor and control this phenomenon.

I am referring to the telegraph. It came on the scene in the 1800's. If you thought I was talking about the Internet, I rest my case. The point is, other generations have also experienced seismic changes in how their world worked – it's not just about us!

The telegraph literally shrank the world. Think about it – news from stock markets, elections, or battlefields could now make its way around the world in minutes, instead of weeks. Business deals across oceans could be negotiated in hours, instead of months.

The Internet allows more, but which invention had the greater impact on their respective generations?

A while back Jay Leno did a bit on his talk show, pitting a couple of expert telegraph operators against a couple of techies, to see if e-mail was faster than the telegraph. Each sent an identical message to his partner. The Morse Code telegraph guys won. It's probably still on You Tube.

A Whole New World

Over the last couple of decades there have been two broad and deep changes transforming our world of work. One, obviously, is technology.

Technology

Technology has had several key impacts. The first is, in the reality of today's world, we don't need to congregate people together anymore for the purpose of getting the work done. This is truer in some instances than in others, and there are certain circumstances where we do need to bring people together. However, the gigantic office buildings of downtown, filled with the rows and rows of desks we've all seen in pictures, were really all about people having access to information. Everyone needed to be in the building because that's where the files were.

Some of us are old enough to remember when memos used to come out almost weekly, describing new procedures for signing files out of the filing room. Keeping track of the files, which had all the information, was a critical, full time job for small armies of people inside any large organization.

Your fathers', or grandfathers', iconic 'Organization Man' of the 50's, and 60's, and the women who supported them (put your hackles back down; that's the way it pretty much was then) could not work anywhere but at the office. That's where everything – all the equipment and all the information – was kept.

Today we don't need to congregate people together to get the work done. With some exceptions, such as physical manufacturing, we can get work done almost anywhere. Perhaps you are one of those exceptions, but for at least part of your job, you have the capacity to work from just about anywhere. You can 'assemble' only at the plant. You can talk and think anywhere.

This is not to suggest that we don't need to congregate people together. All the soft issues of morale, loyalty, creative ideas, and innovative approaches reflect the reality that we work better with people we know. We still need to gather people together for all of those purposes, but we don't need to gather people together to get the work done. In fact, I would suggest that most organizations, if they started today, with a clean piece of paper, would structure their organizations very differently.

People today are living in two different versions of 'normal'.
In one version of 'normal' one gets up at o-dark-hundred, puts on a shirt and tie, or pantyhose, sits on the clogged highway or a crowded bus, pollutes the environment to arrive and pay $28 to

park the car for the day, goes to the office tower that costs $50 a square foot, being visibly there at nine in the morning, remaining until five in the afternoon. The process is then repeated going backwards.

In the other version of 'normal', a person's personal life is almost completely integrated with her business life. In this version, 'work' is not a place; work refers to what you do. In this version, work is totally integrated with the lifestyle and there's no artificial barrier to indicate that work is only done between the hours of nine and five, on set days of the week. She is free to work when she wants or needs to, and at her convenience – the 'when' and 'how' being determined by other things going on in her life. It's an interesting concept and not necessarily a new one.

Think back 125 years ago. When agriculture was the largest employer of the day, families did not feel the need to separate their work from their home life. Ask anyone who grew up in a farm family – mealtime conversations often evolved around work-related issues or concerns. Would the impending storm hold off long enough to harvest the wheat? Would the much needed rain arrive to end the drought that was ruining the crops? Weather, seeding and feeding schedules, animal illnesses, and shifting grain prices, were very much a part of everyday, household conversations. Before the advent of big industrial factories, this is how everyone functioned.

For years, we have been listening to people advising that the secret to success is to separate personal life from work life. This is just silly nonsense. Anyone engaged in brainwork does not leave their brain at work – they bring it home with them and it continues to function long after the 5 o'clock quitting time or, by extension, long before the 9 a.m. start time. This is why it is not uncommon for a person to awaken at 3 a.m., having just sorted through a myriad of information, subconsciously, to arrive at a much-needed solution, resolving an outstanding issue in the workplace.

The secret to success is not separating work and family lives, but rather learning to focus on one area at a time.

When you are at a sporting event, *be there*. Fully. Leave the work worries outside the arena and concentrate on the sporting activity swirling around you. Similarly, when you are in work mode, concentrate fully on the issue at hand, whether conceptualizing the framework needed for a new design project, or scheduling interviews for the top five candidates for 'X' position.

The number of home based businesses has skyrocketed in the last twenty years, many headed by creative women seeking to stay at home with their children while continuing to contribute economically to the family. A combination of several sources suggests that today there are over 40 million homes in the United States today from which income producing work is being done. This has created the second version of 'normal' we see today.

Twenty-five years ago, if you were having a business conversation on the phone and were told, "Hold on, I have to let the dog out," you would have been shocked and would have perceived the individual with whom you were speaking as unprofessional – maybe even thinking that he or she was not really serious about their work or business.

Fast forward to today's work world. Today, a similar conversation probably doesn't even register with you as being anything out of the ordinary. You don't see it as unusual or unprofessional. You may even be impressed with the person's ability to multi-task, and perhaps be a bit envious that the person is at home, getting a load of laundry done while working, apparently having found a way to successfully combine earning a living with a less hectic, more seamless life – one where work and life are not separated but integrated, where the focus on each part of life is at the appropriate time and place. In essence, this 'new normal' lifestyle is one where each aspect (work or family) takes center stage whenever appropriate.

I know people who go to the office for meetings, and regularly spend time working from home so they can "get some work done."

We are only now beginning to see the strategic possibilities of what technology allows us to do. Up until this point, we primarily focused on the tactical mechanics of how to use technology to make things happen much faster.

These are all broad, sweeping statements and there are 100 exceptions to all of them, but this entire shift has been one of the key implications of technology.

A second key impact of technology has been a broad shift to dependence on <u>individual</u> talent. As technology has become better and better, and increasingly sophisticated, dependence on the individual has gone up. There are fewer and fewer people who are in job situations where they have no capacity, as individuals, to impact the outcome the organization is trying to achieve.

There are relatively few jobs left of what was once a huge percentage for the middle class involved in mechanical, assembly line jobs.

We built our organizations around the engineering capacity of the assembly line. Where there was a function that needed to be performed that was too sophisticated for the technology of the moment, we plugged in a person.

These are the jobs with which we are all familiar, and many of us, at some point in our careers, have personally experienced. They require repetitive, physical movement, and very little thought process. Under most organizational structures, no independent thinking is allowed. They are the mind-numbing, soul-destroying jobs of the assembly lines, period. In that environment, no one individual has very much influence on what comes out at the other end. The decision making process and the ability to impact results all reside with the people who design the line, and who design the giant system in which the individual is simply an unthinking, sophisticated piece of machinery.

Technology has helped organizations transition through much of that type of organizational structure. Today there are as many robot trouble-shooters, software experts, etc. on the factory floor as there are traditional factory workers.

There's an old joke about the factory of the future that employs one man and a dog. The man's job is to feed the dog. The dog is there to make sure the man doesn't touch anything.

Technology has also leveled the playing field tremendously. It is now possible for a very tiny number of people, or even just one individual, to compete in many of the knowledge work areas, with large organizations providing similar kinds of services. In this universe, ideas, networks, and individual expertise are everything.

It was not long ago that even a purely white collar, 'nothing but thinking' kind of office needed to be capitalized. Photocopiers, computers, printers, scanners – all of these things cost serious money. (When I started my business in the late 70's, I <u>leased</u> my first answering machine. Younger readers will be stunned by such a thought, perhaps not knowing that answering machines cost $3,000 in those days).

Today you can fully equip an office with much of the same technology the largest global firms have, and you can charge it on your credit card!

As ideas have become paramount, and technology has become cheap, geography has become irrelevant. We are in an age where individual talent rules . . . all over the world.

Globalization

We are all aware of the globalization of our economy over recent years. This is often a political hot button, with many passions in all directions, but nonetheless, it's a reality. This, too, is not a brand new phenomenon.

A century ago, there was actually a greater percentage of the world's GDP involved in global trade than there is today. As ideas have become predominant, as technology has become inexpensive, as communication technology has absolutely exploded, and geography has become irrelevant, the talented and ambitious people, everywhere in the world, have the accessibility to participate in the economy in ways they never could before.

In North America, the upheaval this has caused is a very fundamental shift in the way we look at our place in the world. A similar shift has happened in all the developed economies from Spain to Singapore, Norway to New Zealand, Ireland to Israel, and many places in between. However, particularly in North America, we have seen the end of what might be called 'luxury thinking'. We've had a perception, for a very long time, that the world will buy our products and services and that somehow the money will keep flowing.

An extreme example of this is the implosion of the 'Big 3' North American automobile companies. The industry players spent decades fighting with each other over pieces of a pie they assumed would continue to get larger and larger, despite the rather overwhelming evidence that, in fact, their piece of that pie was getting smaller and smaller.

'Luxury thinking' is not the scandalous greed we saw at the top end of a few organizations over the last few years. (That kind of behavior makes some of us sorry we outlawed public flogging.) I'm referring to a state of mind. Freud coined the wonderful term, "the narcissism of petty differences."

One of the bonuses of my line of work – I'm able to travel a great deal. When you go to a place like Vietnam, as an example, you can talk to the cab driver, the doorman at the hotel, the clerks in the shops – they can all tell you what the goals and the vision are for the country. They can describe in some detail where they're heading and what they need to do to get there.

We, in the developed and historically prosperous economies, have given ourselves over to the assumption that ever-increasing lifestyle, ever-increasing wealth, is somehow part of an inherent birthright. In many cases, we have allowed ourselves to succumb to "the narcissism of petty differences." If all the basics are all looked after and we continue to live well, then we can argue and fuss about the relatively small things as we move forward. That world has been shaken.

One of the realities rolling out of this – we have seen the end of the paternalistic company. There was a time when young graduates were given the well-intended advice, "Get in with a good company; they will look after you."

This advice is comical to someone graduating today. The employer who will look after you, manage your career, look after your pension, etc. is gone. Not gone out of any grand conspiracy of malice, but gone out of the reality that providing those things to employees is no longer affordable.

In its place, we have seen the rise of individual responsibility, not only from a financial sense, but also from a career sense, and from a defining-the-work-we-do sense. We each react to this in our own way. Certainly there is some bad that comes with the good, or good that comes with the bad, but it is a reality of the world in which we're functioning.

This world, while chaotic and frightening to many, is a world of greatly expanded freedoms and possibilities for the overwhelming majority. It's difficult for someone in their 20's today to imagine a time when it was not unusual for a man to be called into the boss's office and told, "Congratulations! You've been appointed the assistant branch manager in Winnipeg!"

It was equally normal that it would be followed by, "Here are your plane tickets; you leave on Monday. Go home, tell the wife, put the house on the market, arrange to get the kids out of school; they'll be joining you in two weeks."

No one ever thought of saying no, and no one thought it was a terribly unusual happening. That was the other side of the paternalistic organization.

Today it is rare, if not an extinct possibility, that any organization would make that announcement as a fait accompli to almost any employee. The question becomes: How do we handle the freedoms and opportunities this new world is creating?

We each have our own reactions to what we see going on. It may well be that it is not right, it is not fair, and it is not just – it just is. This is the reality in which we work. The questions are: How do we adapt to it? How do we make the decisions and take the actions that will allow us to thrive in it, by whatever our personal definition of 'thrive' may be?

Hollywood Days & Cyber Knights

We have moved into what I call the *Age of Hollywood Days and Cyber Knights*. This is the evolution that has transformed 'secretaries' into 'administrative professionals'. (There have been many other factors at play here, but this has been one of the main drivers of this major change that has been happening primarily below the surface).

That was then . . .

We've seen professional associations like The International Association of Administrative Professionals change their focus – from helping their members be great secretaries to helping them become career-minded, administrative professionals. Recognizing this macro-trend is what caused this association, some 15 or 20 years ago, to change its name from Professional Secretaries International to the IAAP.

Not too long ago, all our organizations used to operate as functional silos. Decisions went up the silo, everything got decided at the top, and then decisions went back down the silo. Organizational charts were nice, neat configurations of tiny boxes all linked in vertical rows. They reflected how things happened in the organization. Today's organizations live or die by how well they handle the white space in between the specific job descriptions or job functions on that organizational chart.

Hollywood Days refers to the fact that more and more organizations are recognizing that they are de facto functioning the way Hollywood has always functioned. A disparate group of individuals, with specific skill sets, are brought together for a given period of time, to execute a specific project. Once that project is over, never again does the same team assemble, and certainly not for the same purpose.

Inside our organizations, the demands of the marketplace often mean we can no longer bring innovations – in operations and procedures, or products and markets – to completion, with sufficient speed to remain competitive, by following the old 'up-the-silo-down-the-silo' mechanism for putting new ideas into practice. In organizations of all sizes and sectors, an explosion of project teams, committees, task forces, and working groups, has emerged. These groups cross functional boundaries and hierarchical levels. Only by bringing together all the various stakeholders and influencers can we implement change with the efficiency and speed necessary to keep up with, or ideally stay a step ahead of, others in our marketplace.

Thus, we have a completely new way of working. Gone, for just about everyone, are the days of repetitive, predictable, robotic functions. Instead, we participate in multiple projects, tasks, and a variety of involvements with a larger circle of individuals. It's a significant change from understanding what our 'job' was, to determining and executing what our 'role' is. I refer to this new way of working as *'Hollyworking'*.

The *Cyber Knights* are those people who function well in this new environment. Let me be very specific – this is not referring to a technical skill set. This is all about a headspace, it's all about attitude, it's all about approach, and it's all about how we see ourselves contributing value in the organization. For many newer companies, this has been their 'normal' since the beginning, and they operate almost completely in this fashion. For others, it has been a more gradual change. However, it is not hard to find dozens of people who have a job title that their parents do not understand at all.

It makes sense to understand what the real changes are, where they are coming from, and where they are heading. Before we continue that discussion, let's take a moment and talk about change itself.

Everyone Hates Change

Everyone hates change is one of the common 'truisms' of business life, or maybe life in general. It's a very convenient explanation for why it is difficult to introduce new things into organizations.

It may be convenient, but it is not true.

In fact, it's complete nonsense! We all make changes – dramatic, huge changes; many of which we seek and anticipate with great enthusiasm.

Many of us, at some point, get married. Does that create a significant change in our lives? Probably none bigger. Additionally, we plan for it for months and months, and throw huge parties to celebrate it with all our friends and relatives.
(A friend of mine told me he could have purchased a small car for what he spent on his daughter's wedding. Sadly, the car would have lasted longer!)

Lots of us have children. Does that cause a change in our lives? Wow, if only we'd known . . . and yet, it's another much-anticipated, celebrated change.

People don't hate change. Our concern is the changes we don't understand or for which we cannot see the personal or professional implications. People don't hate change.

We resist the unknown. The changes we look forward to are ones with end results we can picture in our minds. Sometimes these changes don't turn out the way we imagine, but we enter into them with a picture of an end result that we like.

People don't hate change. They fear not knowing where it's going.

We don't hate change; we hate feeling out of control. The changes we celebrate are those we plan for and decide to make for ourselves.

I've never been a great fan of 'change-for-change-sake' inside organizations. I've seen lots of the 'let's shake things up, just to get a change of pace' mentality at work. People new in a position, particularly a managerial one, often instinctively feel a need to reorganize everything on day one . . . with no particular purpose evident to anyone else. Sometimes they'll tell you, "It's good for our folks to get used to change." (As if there isn't enough change going on in most people's lives as it is!)

There's an old story about a newly promoted executive who is replacing someone who was recently terminated. Showing up on her first day, she finds three envelopes on her desk, with a note from the departed predecessor that says, "When you hit a crisis and you have no idea what to do, open envelope #1. If it happens again, open envelope #2. If you hit a third, open envelope #3."

Within a month, the new executive opens the first envelope and reads, "Blame it on me." This strategy works, avoiding blame and buying time.

Some time later the second envelope is opened, revealing, "Reorganize!" This works even better. By distracting everyone, creating lots of busy-ness, and even the illusion of progress, it fills months and months of time.

Eventually, the third envelope is opened. It says, "Prepare three envelopes."

While it is true, not all change creates progress; it is equally true that all progress does create change.

That last sentence may have gone by pretty fast. Think about it: all progress creates change. This is true for your organization, and equally true for you. If you want to build a different future for yourself, you'll need to decide to do some things differently. As the old adage says: "Even if you're on the right track, if you sit still long enough, eventually you'll get run over."

In the vast majority of organizations I've worked with, I've learned if we can make changes that help people to be more effective, if we can make changes that add interest and impact to what people are doing, people enthusiastically embrace those changes. Change can be a great thing if we simply understand some of what, why, and how it affects us.

Birth of the Cyber Knights

This change to the *Age of Hollywood Days and Cyber Knights* started in the late 80's and early 90's, as two converging forces came together. The first was the explosion of accessible technology. As desktop computers became relatively inexpensive and powerful, the capacity to do productive work in the knowledge economy, without large and expensive infrastructure, emerged.

At the same time, a wave of mergers, acquisitions, and economic upheaval led to substantial numbers of layoffs, and the first wave of buyouts, early-outs, golden parachute packages, etc.

It was what we might call the phenomenon of the 'children of the 60's', the middle-core of the baby boom that in huge numbers decided to take the package, and launch into their own microbusinesses. We saw an explosion of one, two, or three-person, knowledge-based businesses, many of them established to serve the new needs of the larger and more traditional organizations, as they adopted new technology.

Some, like computer programmers, networking experts, and website designers, were specifically geared to the new, emerging technologies. Many others found roles in the exploding personal services sector. (An example: the fastest growing occupation in the 1990's was financial planner, almost a non-existent job before then.) The end result – our economy transitioned significantly in the kinds of work being done and who was doing it.

Those who sold individual expertise, and access to their personal networks, exploded from a few million in North America, in the traditional, mandated professions, to dozens of millions making their living in this same fashion. Doctors, lawyers, accountants, and other 'professionals' have always functioned this way. You've experienced it: you go to see the doctor. Your GP refers you to a specialist, who sends you to another specialist, etc.

However, the combination of new technology, economic restructuring, and the mindset of those who came of age during that thing we call the 60's, changed the rules of the game.

The basic rule change was one of control. Whereas long established, well-controlled, mandated governing bodies had determined entry to the traditional professions, the new world was all about individual ability. With very few barriers to entry, anyone with the talent to deliver results was able to join the game.

As the 'children of the 60's' discovered in the 80's and 90's, no one was going to look after their careers except them. They taught their children this same concept, and they taught them well. Those children, now known as the Millennials, approach the workplace with this same philosophy firmly embedded in their psyche.

This change has created the major shift in our world of work over the last several years; it is not just about individuals starting their own businesses. This is a fundamental shift in both the mechanics and the headspace of how we earn a living. This is what the introduction of the knowledge economy looks like.

The Knowledge Economy

We have heard a lot over the years about how the changes we are witnessing from the industrial economy to the knowledge economy are very much like the shift that happened from the agrarian economy to the industrial economy. This is not a very accurate comparison. I believe we are seeing a much larger shift.

In the days of the agrarian economy, the primary asset was land, which was owned by a relatively tiny number of people – usually because someone's ancestor out-fought someone else's ancestor for it. The vast majority of people contributed physical labor to make that asset productive.

In the industrial economy, the primary asset was machinery. The capital to build the factories allowed us to create something of value. A relatively small number of people owned this as well, and the vast majority of us contributed physical labor to make that asset productive.

In the knowledge economy, the key assets are creativity, innovative thinking, networks of resources, and the capacity to learn new and different ways of doing things. These assets are owned by, or at least available to, virtually everyone who chooses to recognize and use them.

This is a much more fundamental re-thinking of how our world of work is structured and functions. It is really a shift in what the Germans call 'weltanschuang', which is the whole worldview of how things hang together. In looking for a historic parallel, we need to look back to the shift from city-states to nation-states that happened in Europe centuries ago, eventually creating modern countries such as Germany, France, and England.

How do we best take advantage of this new reality?

The Cyber Knights

While we have seen an explosion in actual micro-businesses, this *Age of Hollywood Days and Cyber Knights*, this universe of *'Hollyworking'*, is not only the reality outside our organizations; it is also a mindset inside our organizations.

Both internal and external *Cyber Knights* have one, overriding characteristic in common – they see themselves as solution partners.

I don't mean this in the sense of the software industry terminology, but in a sense that says, "If we have moved to a world where I don't need administrative help to type a letter or take phone messages, (and lots still do this, but they don't NEED to do it anymore), then what is it our organizations need us to do?"

This shift is a big part of the shift happening inside the administrative segments of our organizations. A shift from the manufacturing universe where everybody was told what to do by somebody – probably told exactly how to do it, and then 'supervised' to make sure they were doing it – to a world that says, "Understand what's going on around you and why. Then make yourself useful to help it happen more effectively."

Key attributes that effective *Cyber Knights* have in common inside their workplace:

- **Career managers**

They clearly understand that no one will look after their career for them. They know they are responsible for their own career. They give serious thought to where they want to be and how they are going to get there.

- **Opportunity seekers and idea generators**

They consciously seek out opportunities to shine. They contribute by generating new ideas or concepts that will move the company closer its goals.

- **Constant horizon scanners**

They always have their radar turned on, constantly scanning the environment, paying attention to what is going on around them, absorbing information, recognizing trends, and using this knowledge for themselves and their careers, as well as for the company's well-being.

- **Multi-taskers and team players**

They are comfortable volunteering to take on additional projects and tasks, recognizing that in doing so they are seen as good team players. They develop personal contacts, refine their interpersonal skills, and gain subject matter expertise to add to the office environment and on their resumes. They are good at handling multiple priorities and changing work groups.

- **Skill set self-reliant**

They maintain their skills to match current requirements and emerging trends. They do not sit back and wait to acquire these skills. They understand they are responsible for acquiring the skills needed for success at any point in time.

- **Project focused; results driven**
They understand that work today is evolving, often characterized by project work involving people being brought together for a pre-determined length of time, to complete a specific assignment. They are focused on delivering results, not being bogged down in procedures, politics, and precedents. They understand each project gives them the opportunity to acquire more knowledge, develop new skills, and/or refine existing ones. They understand volunteering to work on a project is one way to be 'in the know', while creating a profile within the company and expanding one's support network.

- **Impact obsessed**
They work hard to understand how what they do contributes to the big picture. Specifically their mission is to know how what they do can impact the organization and make it better.

- **Connected and networked**
They know nothing gets accomplished without people. They actively work to develop personal networks of supportive colleagues. This helps them understand what is happening around them and what it means both for the organization and for their careers. They know who can bring what information, attributes, and attitudes to the party to make things happen. (APs are often ideally suited to be able to 'find answers' because of their natural networks throughout the organization).

- ***Received an A+ in 'Works and plays well with others'***
  They have excellent interpersonal skills and are especially adept at getting along with everyone they connect with in their day-to-day work. They comfortably interact with people at all levels of the organization and are valuable contributors to committees or project teams.

Rob Hosking, Executive Director of Office Team, notes that while technical expertise is important, "The ability to collaborate and build consensus on projects distinguishes top performers."

On the following pages are some simple charts to help you think about where you are at this moment, and where the organization you currently working for fits in the context of this discussion.

These are not designed to be highly sophisticated, elaborate 'tests' of anything. They're just a way for you to take a quick snapshot of this moment in time before we move on.

A handy summary checklist of Cyber Knight characteristics: Where would you put yourself at this point in time?

Cyber Knight Characteristics:	1 Poor	2 Fair	3 Good	4 Very Good	5 Excellent
Career Manager					
Opportunity Seeker & Idea Generator					
Career & Company Horizon Scanner					
Multi-tasker & Team Player					
Skill Set Self-Reliant					
Project Focused & Results Driven					
Impact Obsessed					
Connected & Networked					
A+ in "works and plays well with others"					

What does your score mean?

Total Score	Action Plan
35 to 45	Congratulate yourself for belonging to the Order of Cyber Knights. You obviously understand the skills needed for success in today's working world.
25 to 34	You are a Cyber Knight in training. Continue to acquire and practice new skills, and you will soon earn your shield.
10 to 24	You have heard tales about the Cyber Knights and are wandering the countryside hoping to catch a glimpse of these fabled creatures. Look for find them and quickly embrace their way of thinking and acting.
0 to 9	You are waiting for a knight in shining armor to rescue you. This is not going to happen, so be very nice to your current boss. The only person who can rescue you, is you. Think about taking the initiative to learn some new skills so you too can thrive in today's world of Cyber Knights.

How Cyber Knight-friendly is your current workplace?

Is your company a good place for Cyber Knights?	1 Poor	2 Fair	3 Good	4 Very Good	5 Excellent
Genuinely welcomes employees' ideas and suggestions					
Utilizes multiple communication vehicles, to ensure understanding of the company 'big picture', vision, & goals					
Spends energy & time breaking down &/or preventing silos					
Supports & encourages employees to acquire new skills					
Has cross-functional committees, working groups, task forces and special project teams					
Endorses flexible work arrangements: e.g. telecommuting & compressed weeks					
Expects all employees to think, show initiative, & independently resolve day-to-day issues					

What does your organization's score mean?

Total Score	Action Plan
25 to 35	Congratulate yourself for working in a company that understands how to keep Cyber Knights happy and well fed
15 to 24	The company is aware that Cyber Knights exist and is attempting to join the world of Cyber Knights. The company will be in danger of decreasing sales and profits if it does not give quick and proper attention to all efforts and changing skills needed to be successful in the battlefield.
0 to 14	Like dinosaurs, the company will eventually become extinct. This is especially true if they are in a competitive marketplace where their customers have many choices.

A World of Possibilities

I am absolutely convinced that we are moving into a day and age where more people, from more places, and more backgrounds, are going to have more opportunity, to do more things, that are more fun, and more lucrative, than we have ever experienced in the history of humankind.

Activity vs. Results

One obvious manifestation inside organizations of the *Age of Hollywood Days and Cyber Knights*, is a fundamental shift in what we expect people to do and how we go about evaluating how they are doing it. Basically, we have moved from an age of *activity* to an age of *results*.

At one point in time, somebody could look at you and tell if you were being productive. If you were leaning on your shovel, you weren't being productive. If you were sitting at your keyboard and your fingers weren't moving, you weren't being productive.

That age is largely gone. In a world where it's all about figuring out better ways to do things; understanding strategic intent; accurately reflecting values; sorting priorities; facilitating interaction among various components; solving problems – it's increasingly difficult to look at anybody and determine whether or not they are being productive.

In the age of activity, management was a relatively simple function. We hired people to watch people to see whether or not they were being productive. If they weren't, someone went over and poked them with stick and told them to get busy. These folks were called overseers because, quite literally, that's what they were. Their job was to watch people to see if they were working. We thought the term 'overseer' was a little harsh, so we reverted to Latin and called them 'super-visors'.

It is almost amusing to think there was an age when we used to pay people based on how long their body was physically inside the building. We used to punch people in and out on a big clock on the wall, monitor their time by the minute, and then it was someone else's job to make them productive while they were there.

We have now moved to an age of results.

The age of results reflects a philosophy that says, "Here's what I need to get done. Within these parameters of time, or cost, or quality, here's what I need to have happen. I don't care where you do it, when you do it, how you do it, or who you do it with; these are the results I need, within these given parameters. This is not about me designing a system in detailed mechanics for you to blindly follow. It's about you understanding the end result I need to have happen, and then having, or finding, and using, sufficient insight and information to determine how to make it happen."

We see this same trend challenging education systems in all the developed economies around the world. We have education systems fundamentally designed to prepare our kids to 'get a job'. The reality is, there are fewer and fewer jobs. There's lots of work, but there are fewer and fewer 'jobs'.

What we need are education systems designed to prepare our kids to create a living for themselves – to find something they are good at, something they enjoy doing, then to acquire the skills to do it very well, and with the ability to package that skill set in such a fashion they can sell it to somebody.

This is very much what we see happening inside organizations as well. Career-minded professionals are concentrating on understanding what they are particularly good at and enjoy; determining how they can package and present those capabilities to build their desired futures, starting inside their current organizations.

This is very different than waiting for the next promotion. You can't move up a job ladder when there is no ladder.

Stop waiting for somebody to put the ladder back; start looking at how you can most effectively build your own ladder. Build it and put it up against whatever wall you choose.

Everybody has Customers

You have customers. No matter what position you're in, no matter what it is you are doing, you have customers. Somebody uses the results of your efforts. (If this does not happen be true for you at this particular moment, I strongly recommend you do whatever you need to do to change this, before someone else notices that no one uses anything you do.) Whoever uses the results of your efforts, is your customer.

There was a point in time when secretaries had one customer – the boss. Today administrative professionals have a huge variety of entities inside an organization that are their customers. Managing a project, or any other kind of support function, is all about defining the 'within these parameters' part of getting things done, so that everyone who needs to understand it, does.

This transition to the universe of *'Hollyworking'*, the *Age of Hollywood Days and Cyber Knights*, means there is substantially more need for coordinators, catalysts, and facilitators. I don't mean facilitators in the 'stand at the flip chart during the meeting' common usage, but in its real definition from the French, 'facile':

the role is 'to make easy' or 'to make simple'. That's what we're looking for administrative professionals to do, no matter what aspect of the organization they spearhead, coordinate, or support. This means we need to know more things, we need to know different things, and we need to use different skill sets.

There are a whole lot of good news / bad news stories here. The news itself is neither good nor bad, its just news. Whether it's good or bad depends on the context in which you choose to hear it and what you choose to do with it.

The fact that everyone has customers means that there's a market out there for everyone. However, what those customers are wanting, and willing to pay for is constantly changing.

Rob Hosking again: "Administrative professionals are being relied on more than ever to manage budgets, negotiate vendor contracts, oversee projects, and maintain websites, in addition to their more traditional responsibilities."

The bad news is that the traditional role administrative professionals have played in organizations is shrinking, if not disappearing. The good news is the underlying skill set they bring to the table will continue to be in demand. However, it will only be in demand for those who know how to augment it and package it to be of value to their customers.

We're all aware that health care and the hard sciences are two occupational areas that will continue to grow dramatically over the next decade. Another sector seeing explosive growth is the business and professional services sector. This is obviously a large umbrella. The World Future Society refers to this as "the most severe shortage of skilled workers in history." It goes on to say, "This sellers market for labor will give sought after specialists the privilege of designing their jobs to fit their own preferences." We are talking growth in the order of millions of new jobs.

These new jobs will look quite different from traditional jobs. Those jobs that involved routine or rote activities, done day after day, in return for a simple annual compensation, are disappearing. This shift in jobs is not new. If we look across the last decade or two, we have huge percentages of our workforce currently employed in jobs that didn't even exist 10, 15, or 20 years ago. This transition will continue to accelerate.

New jobs will be created to respond to new needs inside our organizations. Those who thrive in this environment will be those with a broad awareness of what's going on, and the ambition and creativity to respond to evolving and emerging needs. The adage is true in today's workplace: "If you behave like a robot, you risk being replaced by one." Machines are good at efficiency; they cannot think. Those who can will carve new futures for themselves.

Brenda Barnes is the Chairman and CEO of Sara Lee. *Fortune* magazine lists her at the #9 spot in the *2008 Most Powerful Women in Business* issue. She says, " My advice to young people would be to actively manage your career. No one will care more about it than you do." This is great advice because no one is going to step up and offer you your super, ideal job. You will have to create it for yourself.

Here's a fun way to see how we are scrambling to keep up with this transition. All of us understand what a job description of 'Computer Doctor' might entail: obviously someone who solves computer problems. However, if you go to monster.com or hotjobs.com, the gigantic job sites, and search 'computer doctor' you get no exact matches (only medical-related, 'both-word' hits). If, on the other hand, you go to the vernacular source and punch 'computer doctor' into Google, you'll see 111,000 hits. Our intuitive understanding of what is going on is way ahead of the formal structures!

As we are swamped with data, our appetite for information continues to grow. As our business networks expand and become more complex, the need for those who can keep the networks linked and make the relationships function, will also continue to grow. Many of these jobs will be as facilitators, aggregators, and coordinators for new and emerging needs inside our organizations.

Some jobs will require technical capability. (This is great for administrative professionals: IAAP and *Office Team* surveys say 95% find it easy to adapt to new technology). Many more will depend on a top-notch set of the 'soft skills' that make organizations work well.

Here is a sampling of the kinds of job titles we'll see becoming more commonplace in the next few years:

- Global Work Process Coordinator
- Corporate Alumni Director
- Imaging Specialist
- Logistics Coordinator
- Project Coordinator
- Central Resources Coordinator
- Presentation/Graphics Coordinator
- Software Trainer
- Virtual Resources Coordinator
- Software Adaptor
- Website Maintainer (updater)
- Online Purchaser
- Desktop Publisher
- Home-based Administrative Services
- Information Management on the Web
- Internal Systems Troubleshooter
- Creating Customized Software Manuals
- Newsletter Editor
- Multimedia Librarian/Information Abstractor
- Video Conferencing Coordinator
- Technology Coordinator
- Graphics and Desktop Publishing Coordinator
- Blog Tracker and Disseminator / Responder

Let's take one of these job titles and see if it is real – Corporate Alumni Director. What the heck is that?

There is a fast growing group of companies who recognize that a key element of their soft, influencer network falls under the category of what universities refer to as 'alumni'. In this case, people who once worked there and now work elsewhere. They understand that part of their ongoing success is the ability to maintain relationships with people they know.

I've known numerous executives, in a variety of businesses, who, after graduation, went to work for McKinsey, a huge global consulting firm. These people received their degrees at places like Harvard and Stanford and other top tier universities around the world. They unanimously tell me that the most frequent and most effective alumni communication they receive is from McKinsey, their former employer, not from their educational alma maters.

Jeffrey Katzenberg, the CEO of DreamWorks Animation, says, "We have alumni from roughly a dozen great art schools around the country. We send people back to lecture; we invite the teaching staff to tour and see what we're doing, with the idea that their curriculum can be fitted to our needs; we partner with higher education so they'll want to produce talent that is valuable to us." Someone needs to discover, coordinate, communicate, and organize all of these activities on behalf of both of these organizations.

There are dozens of organizations like DreamWorks, and this position will become more common in organizations of all sizes. Someone will have to figure out how to do it effectively.

The Economy in 2009

Recession: *n*
A re-distributive period, during which the market takes from both the timid and the scared, and gives to the creative, and to the bold.

As I write this, in mid-2009, economic times are tough. Perhaps all this talk of new jobs and the changing world of work seems inappropriate when the news suggests the stress level is all about just hanging on to any job.

The headlines tell us the unemployment rate in much of the developed world has doubled from around 5% to someplace close to 10%. There are those for whom this is creating genuine stress and there will be those who go through some very tough times. In the larger picture, it is worthwhile to keep in mind, that what this means is that nine out of ten people in the workforce are still employed, which is not as good as nine and a half, but is still a 90% employment rate.

(The *Economist* magazine reports that on average about 15% of jobs in America disappear every year. In boom times, these are all replaced with new jobs as the economy evolves. In tough times, fewer of them are replaced, and certainly not as quickly. Other less turbulent economies have smaller numbers, but it is an ongoing process everywhere in the developed world.)

We know two things:

First, just as good times eventually come to an end, so do bad times. Across the last 150 years, market economies have spent between 7% and 15% of the time in some sort of economic upheaval. There will be a tomorrow, the sun will rise, and things will start moving forward and growing again.

Secondly, within a year or two of the upturn, the pecking order in almost every industry and market will have changed.

I have been telling corporate, executive audiences, "For many, the biggest danger of this recession is that it will not last long enough."

Why? Because right now, there are two kinds of organizations:

There are those that are 100% focused on the next three or six months, to the exclusion of all else. While it makes perfect sense to be doing the things that need to be done to get the organization through these tough times, there are also many organizations taking another approach.

They are spending 10% to 20% of their time figuring out how to restructure, how to reorganize, innovate appropriately, and invest wisely so they are in a position to leapfrog their competition when the markets turn around.

Exactly the same thing is true for individuals. There are those spending their time hand wringing and teeth grinding over the immediate big picture; there are those who will take this moment to rethink what they do, how they do it, why they do it, and begin preparing for new opportunities. For some people, just as for some organizations, the bigger danger is that this recession will not last long enough for them to get ready to thrive when it ends.

Now may not be the ideal time to build your new future. It is, however, the time to design it, gather the materials, and start laying the foundation.

An ancient truth: "When is the best time to plant an oak tree? Thirty years ago. When is the second best time? Today."

Here's a bit of fun for those feeling particularly stressed right now.

ANTI-STRESS DIET	
Diet designed to help you cope with daily stress	
BREAKFAST	LUNCH
½ grapefruit	4 oz lean, broiled chicken breast
1 slice whole wheat toast, dry	1 cup steamed spinach
	1 cup herb tea
8 oz skim milk	1 Oreo cookie
MID AFTERNOON SNACK	DINNER
Rest of the Oreos in the package	3 loaves garlic bread with cheese
2 pints Rocky Road ice cream	Large sausage, mushroom, &
1 jar hot fudge sauce	cheese pizza
Nuts, cherries, whipped cream	4 cans or large pitcher of Pepsi
	3 Milky Way or Snickers bars
LATE EVENING NEWS	
Entire frozen cheesecake direct from the freezer	

Building Your Own Future

Skill Set Self-Reliance

Skill set self-reliance is an interesting *Cyber Knight* characteristic. In one sense it's a bit of a head-nodder – of course, you need to know what you need to know, to do what you need to do. In another sense, it can be a bit of a head-twister. Here's a typical conversation:

"Are you skill set self-reliant?"

"Yes, of course I am. I know how to do all the elements of my job, and do them well."

"What do you know how to do now, that you didn't know how to do six months ago? What have you learned that's new this year?"

"Well, times are tough, our training budget has been cut, and I haven't been sent on any training programs for quite a while."
"What have you sent yourself on?"

"Uh . . . " now it gets sticky!

In this new *Age of Hollywood Days and Cyber Knights*, we need to be responsible for building the skill sets that will allow us to function successfully in the job we want to have. This is what being skill set self-reliant is all about.

The old days of, "If the company expected me to know how to do that, they would have sent me on a training program" are gone. If not completely gone, they are fading fast. In the days when the company managed your career and you turned it over to them, and they determined how you acquired what skills, for its immediate purposes, this all worked.

Today everyone's primary job is to figure out how to continue to be useful for what the organization will need next. We are all responsible for managing our own careers. We need to be pro-active in identifying and acquiring the knowledge and skills we'll need to accomplish our own career objectives.

It's interesting to note that people will invest thousands and thousands of dollars, and thousands of evening and weekend hours to acquire a college degree to help them get a better job. (Please don't misunderstand me, I am all in favor of additional education, and college degrees are a good thing. I salute those with the ambition and discipline to successfully execute such a plan). Yet, there are many people who would never consider spending a few hours and a few hundred dollars to take a course of some sort to help them be more effective in the job they are doing now. (I've met people who won't invest $30 in a book that might help them get better!).

Another twist on the old traditional mindset about training: "If I'm going to acquire new skills that will benefit the company, then the company should pay for that."

A different headspace says, "All of us, in whatever capacity, sell our time, our effort, and our knowledge to someone for some amount. The more knowledge we have, the more our time and effort are worth. If I am to continue to be of maximum value to any organization, including the one I am with right now, it is incumbent on me to ensure I contribute a world class set of skills to compliment my time and my effort." This needs to be neither wildly expensive nor dramatically different than what you are currently doing.

Gini Courter is a well-known person to the AP community, and a world class expert in helping you get additional productivity out of the software you already have and use. She will tell you that in most administrative settings, people could be 20%, 30%, or even 50% more productive, if they simply knew how to use all the functionality that is built into the software they already own.

Far too many of us are like the carpenter who learned to drive nails but apparently never figured out that a hammer could also be used for pulling the nails out. This would not be considered a world class, professional, master carpenter, and yet many of us who deal with basic software suites, are in the same boat.

It is one thing to know how to use only 10% of what your TV remote or your mobile phone can do. It is quite another to know how to use only a small percentage of your professional tools.

The question is: Whose job is it to learn how to use his/her professional tools?

Over the last several years, various professional publications have surveyed administrative professionals and the executives they work with to determine what trends are real and where the future lies for the administrative professional.

One such article from *Office Pro* magazine surveyed administrative professionals about how they thought their jobs would change.

The findings that jumped out at me:

- 14% said more management skills are being required
- 19% agreed that more independent thinking is required

In a management survey by Office Team, a leading, international staffing agency, managers said:

- 63% agreed that administrative professionals will be relied on more for project management
- 91% agreed that administrative professionals will have more authority to make decisions

Call me naïve, but there seems to be a bit of a disconnect here: 14% of APs think they need management skills; 63% of their bosses want to see those skills in action. Independent thinking: 19% vs. 91%. Golly.

OK, some of this may be interpretation of the question, sampling of participants, timing, data crunching techniques, etc. Nevertheless, those are huge gaps on very basic issues.

My advice is to make sure you are not inadvertently in that gap. If you want to be able to build your own future, maybe it's time to schedule a candid, cards-face-up meeting with your manager, share these results, and talk about perceptions and expectations.

The *Office Pro* survey lists the following skills and attributes as coming into high demand:

- The ability to get results
- Acting autonomously, making decisions independently
- Having a broad skill set
- Strong self management, and coordinating well with others
- Being open minded, flexible, and easily shifting gears
- Finding more efficient and innovative ways to do the job, and contributing ideas for improving the whole office
- And, predictably, the desire to give 100% at work

Here's a practical tip. It's a plan one person I know made to help them to "give 100% at work" every week:

- ☺ 12% on Monday
- ☺ 23% on Tuesday
- ☺ 40% on Wednesday
- ☺ 20% on Thursday
- ☺ 5% on Friday

Quite seriously, to thrive in this new world of work, you must not only be responsible for what you do, but you need to take responsibility for helping design and define what you do.

By understanding what is happening and why, and learning a bit about some of the trends that are impacting your organization, you are much better prepared to determine what else you're going to need to learn to do, and how you need to get better at what you do.

In an even broader sense, have you read a book on how to persuasively deliver your ideas?

Have you used worksheets or software allowing you to more effectively and more productively organize your time?

Are you aware of your organization's strategic priorities and the specific issues and challenges it is dealing with?

You can't recognize the opportunities in the landscape if you can't see the landscape. (Good for you for having this book in your hands!)

Now, let's talk a bit about what you do with this skill set once you've got it.

Making a Plan

There are five basic options you can pursue for your career:

1. Expand, augment, and/or enhance the job you are currently doing.

2. Find, or create, a new job with your current client. (Yes, I said 'client' on purpose. You can call them 'employer' if you choose, but they are the entity currently buying your services. This is a real head-twister for some, but I promise you it is a helpful thinking habit to get into!)

3. Find a similar job to the one you have now with a new organization.

4. Find a different job with a different organization.

5. Launch out on our own as an independent contractor, selling your services to a variety of client entities.

Most will not do the latter, for lots of reasons. However, if that is the route that makes the most sense for you, you have much more to consider, but most of what follows still applies. So, let's focus on the first four.

Whichever of these is right for you, there are some basics common to just about everyone that succeeds at any of them.

First (and this sounds almost silly), is to decide. It is difficult to successfully execute a plan, if we're not really sure what the plan is. I'm always surprised at the number of people I meet who tell me that they want to make a change, but are unable to articulate what it is they want to change *to*. It is a lot easier to change – happily – *to* something than to just change *from* something.

I'm not going to lecture here about goal setting (there are lots of folks doing that), but really – if you want to make changes or improvements in whatever it is you do to earn your daily bread, how will you tell you've succeeded?

What is it you want? ("Not this!" is not a good enough answer.)

Make some decisions, and then make a plan.

Start with what your 'next' job will look like.

'Next' may very well be the one you have now, with a few modifications. Or it may be something totally new and different. That doesn't matter. What matters is that *you* know what it looks like.

Do this by describing, in writing (If it's not written, it doesn't count!), the characteristics of the job you want to be doing three months, six months, or a year from now. Pick the handful of criteria most important to you. Which ones will most enhance your career satisfaction and enjoyment?

Try writing sentences that start:
    My next job will give me . . .
    My next job will let me . . .
    My next job will make me . . .

Some have found it useful to also have a sentence that starts:
> It will continue to provide me . . .

and then add in what you like best about what you're doing now.

The next steps of the process are deceptively simple, or at least simple sounding.

Having the attributes of your ideal job defined, think through the characteristics, and then through the specific skill sets someone needs to succeed in this job.

Check yourself, today, against that list.

What new skills do you need to acquire (if any)?

What kinds of experience will help persuade someone you are the right person for this job?

A thought many overlook – volunteer activities can help you acquire skills you need, or refine the ones you have. If you need to demonstrate you can run a project team, volunteer to chair a fund-raising initiative, or a membership drive. Volunteer activities are a great place to learn and demonstrate leadership ability (the bonus – they showcase your talents to another network of people).

How will the person effectively doing your ideal job approach the world?

This is tough, but the 'soft' things like attitude, personality, and general behavior in the work environment are all a big part of doing any job well. You know this; you see it all the time.

Hard questions: How are you doing in this department? Does anything need to change?

Here's another idea others have found useful. It's a way to make the little changes that will help on a day-to-day basis.

Pick two changes that could help you – one that you're going to do more of or start doing; the other that you're going to do less of or stop altogether.

Figure out a way to remind yourself of these two things every day. Revisit them every few weeks, and when you've successfully made a new habit of them, pick another two.

People will notice. It will take a little time, but you'll be surprised at how quickly peoples' perceptions can be updated.

Now you have identified your ideal job, the elements needed to succeed, and you have a picture of where you are right now and what you need to do to get ready for it.

A caveat: I've known several who have gone through this exercise and concluded they already have an absolutely terrific job, giving them everything they really need and want right now. One asked me, "What should I do now?"

I said, "Now that you *know* you have the job you really want, enjoy it more!" I wasn't being flippant. It is so easy to think the grass is always greener, to be bogged down in the little things that irritate us; it's useful to remind ourselves to see the bigger picture and enjoy everything that's going right. Put a little note on the bathroom mirror that says, "I've already got it." Remind yourself every day, and it's easier to let it show for everyone else every day.

If you conclude you're already there, focus on getting better, and remember to enjoy it more!

If some sort of a change is in order, you are now in a position to make a plan to get the 'next' job you want.

Another caveat (already!): no plan you make need be cast in concrete for all time. A plan is a place to start – a *way to get started*. It can change, and probably will. There is an old maxim in the military: "No battle plan ever survives first contact with the enemy." While we don't have enemies in building our own future, the concept holds true.

Circumstances change, companies evolve, people come and go, options disappear, and new opportunities arise. Your ideas of what a successful outcome will look like may change too. Now that you have a description of what the end result is supposed to look like, here's the basic sequence of searching for your next, super job.

Can you make your current job into what you want?

Can you find your 'next' in your current organization somewhere?

Can you create it in your current organization?

Are you going to need to go elsewhere?

Whatever the answer is for you, here's a good piece of advice I got years ago that fits: "Look, and sound, and act like you already have it."

In my career, I've seen this over and over in huge, medium-sized, and small organizations, in the private and public sectors, and everywhere in between. One of the keys to getting to where you want to be is already looking like you'll fit in there.

You've seen it too. A new person joins the department, and in short order there is a consensus that 'here's someone who is going places'. She just has 'something'. It's often hard to put a finger on exactly, but everyone seems to know it is there.

One very common factor at work here is this person carries herself as though she is ready for the next move.

This is one of the thought processes to consider in the 'things I may want to change' category we talked about earlier.

Here's some thought starters:

How do you look?
Let's face it; we all have a tendency to get comfortable in our positions. How much of what you usually wear to work would make the cut for 'my first three days on a new job' list? I'm not talking a big money, massive makeover effort here, just suggesting this is worth thinking about, and perhaps a small investment in this area may have big career payoffs.

How do you sound?
Are you habitually solution focused? Does everyone know you cannot be sucked into playing the blame game? Do you see the big picture of what the end result is supposed to be for whatever activities you're handling? How do you talk about the head office, other departments, clients, or suppliers?

How do you act?
What kinds of issues cause you to get angry? Are they big or small? (Someone once said: "You are known by the size of the issues that concern you." A powerful behavior compass!)

Are you the calm in the center of the storm, or part of the storm?

Can you be enticed into a little gossip-fest in the lunchroom, or does everyone know you won't participate?

Are you confident in your abilities and knowledge? Do you state your opinions in a way that reflects confidence, or have you fallen victim to the habit of including strings of qualifiers and disclaimers around every statement of opinion or advice? ("Well, it's only my opinion but I think . . ."; ". . . of course that's just what I think, and I may well be wrong").

This section could go on for a hundred pages, but the intent is simply to provide a few practical ideas to help you get ready to move forward.

Going for It

When you're ready to move forward, here's a good sequence to help you get where you want to be:

First, exhaust your internal possibilities. Unless you have decided you really need to get out of the organization you work for now (the industry is in a death spiral, you need to change geography, or you simply do not want to follow where this management is leading, etc), this is logically your best bet.

Plan B can be to go outside if this doesn't work out, but it's worth investing some effort within your current organization first.

You are already a known entity, and you know the organization and the personalities.

There are almost always more opportunities than are obvious at first glance. No smart company is prepared to lose knowledgeable, contributing people (or wants to find and train new ones) just because someone wants to contribute in a different way.

Making it happen is often about personal confidence, and the willingness to act on it. This can be summed up by the highly technical, human, psycho-behavioral characteristic of 'gumption'. Earlier we said you would have to go after it. This is where that happens, and here's how to do it.

When you find (or make!) the opportunity you want, do these four things to make the pitch to whoever can approve your next job:

1. Describe the problem someone doing your 'next' job will solve. Focus on solutions. Demonstrate you understand the big picture, and describe how what you are proposing will better help whoever is responsible achieve her results.

2. Describe your new job. "People buy things they think they understand" is one of the old maxims of selling. If you're asking someone to move from something they know and understand to something that is less 'knowable', paint a sufficiently detailed picture so they can see how the new idea will work. This demonstrates that you've thought it through, and have a good understanding of how to make it work.

3. Describe your fit for this job. Identify the skill set needed to do this job well, both the hard technical skills and the equally critical, soft skills. Summarize how your skills and experience match what the job requires. Remember to show how you can contribute quickly – you already know the routines, the values, the history, the personalities, and

all the other things that will help this succeed (and that it will take a new person months to learn).

An important note here: this is no time to be shy! A colleague from my consulting firm had a wonderful expression. He used to say, "If you can do it, it ain't braggin'."

Sometimes it's awkward talking about yourself in this way, especially to people you work with and know well. You think 'they know all about me, I don't need to tell them ...'.

When you're asking others to see you in a new light, it makes sense to help them do that. Familiarity breeds, among other things, filters. All of us tend to put people we know in categories, or boxes, and leave them there.

We experience this phenomenon most starkly at events like big family gatherings, or high school reunions. No matter what 'little Bobby' has accomplished in his life . . . and he is now 47-year old Robert to his employees . . . when the family all gets together, he is still 'little Bobby' to them.

Despite the fact that Nancy has gone on to become a world class cardiac surgeon, at the high school reunion she is still seen as that 'geeky' girl, with the weird glasses, in the fourth row. It's human nature.

People change and grow over time. Often we need someone to pull off the old filters to put new ones on. That's what this is about.

If you interview at a new company, you're prepared to talk about your accomplishments and tell them quite specifically what skills you bring to the party. Do the same thing here (this is part of what 'gumption' and 'going after it' looks like!).

4. Describe how you will replace yourself. This is 'solutions thinking'. Don't just arrive with a solution to one problem that creates another problem. (How will what you are currently doing get done?) Solve that one too.

5. You can find, or train, or mentor a new person. Perhaps you can farm out various pieces of what you will no longer be doing to a variety of people and then play a supervisory role to make sure it all gets done smoothly.

This will be a concern to anyone approving your plan; think it through and offer solutions for that too. It's an important part of them being able to envision your idea in action.

Start off the conversation with something along these lines: "I've been thinking seriously for some time now about where I'm going in my career, and what I want to be doing a year from now. I've come to some conclusions, and the first is I'd much prefer to be doing it here."

The idea is to make sure they cannot jump to a conclusion that this is one of those having-a-bad-day-so-they-thought-they'd-take-a-flyer kinds of scenarios. Make it obvious you are serious about your plans for yourself.

As you approach this keep in mind, they want to keep you as much as you want to stay. You are already a proven, valuable contributor to the organization. They can find a new you, but the abilities, personality, attitude, and 'fit' of a new person are unknown.

Taking the initiative to change your role, or find a new role, in your organization is like going to Las Vegas if the rules say you can either win or breakeven. At best, you get exactly what you want. At worst, you're where you are right now. (If you work for a person or an organization that's going to fire you for expressing a desire to move ahead in your career, you need to get out of there in a big hurry anyway!)

Have this conversation with everyone that can help you accomplish your goals. The more people there are who know what you want, the greater the odds someone will recognize the kind of opportunity you are seeking. This is the same reason, when looking outside, for telling your friends, relatives, neighbors, charity and sports networks – everyone you know – what you are looking for. The more 'searchers' you have, the better your odds.

And you may have to go outside. The inside plan may not work. You may need to get to a completely new group of people who can see you fitting the role you want.

If your preference is to stay with your current organization, have some patience and exhaust all possibilities before assuming you must leave to get where you want to go. Give them a fair shot at helping you create your next job, but do so with some time limit in your own mind.

Now you just need the 'gumption' to go after it.

There was an Administrative Professional named Pat who saw, and then had the 'gumption', to seize an opportunity. Pat was going crazy scheduling interviews. A new person was being hired to reorganize a small team that interfaced administratively with several other parts of the company. What was driving Pat crazy was a conviction that reorganizing this group was not going to solve the problem.

One day Pat said to the 'boss' doing the interviewing, "I have scheduled the next 15 minutes for you and I to talk about this hiring process."

"I have been giving this some serious thought. There seems to be a consensus that the problem is structural. I believe it's primarily a procedural problem, not a structural one."

"What you really need in this position is someone who can streamline, and make much more efficient, the processes the team is trying to execute." Pat then gave one specific example of repetitious data entry that was generating numerous errors, causing all kinds of additional work to retroactively correct them.

"Sometimes, Boss, the solution can be found in-house – in this case it's right under your nose. I am the ideal candidate for this job, and here's why. I know the operation well, and the people. You and I already know each other, and we work well together. You'll save the disruption of reorganizing, and the learning curve for a new person. At best, you'll get a faster, smoother, and cheaper solution implemented internally. At worst, you'll get a more efficient, cost-effective operation that it may make sense to reorganize down the road."

"I'll do the preliminary interviews for you for someone to replace me. I know what you need as well as you do. When you choose someone, I will train her, and be here to help her as she gets up to speed."

Pat's boss was a little taken aback, and said, "Let me think on it."

A few days later he came back to Pat saying, "I've decided your approach makes sense, and I must admit I like your moxie. (Who says 'moxie' any more?) So, I've decided to give you a shot at it."

The move ended up opening a completely new career path for Pat. And it all started with Pat having the 'gumption' to go for it.

Going for 'it' is a lot easier if you have a good understanding of the forces that are impacting all our organizations. Use this information when looking at a potential work environment – is this a good place to invest the future of my career?

Look at the following macro-trends, and what they mean for our organizations, our markets, our world of work, and building our own futures.

The Macro Trends

A disclaimer as we dive into all these trends: I'm going to give lots of examples, from lots of different organizations, of all different sizes, in all different sectors, all around the world.

Let me be explicit – I am not endorsing any of these organizations, their products or services; nor am I trying to suggest that their leaders are paragons of virtue. My purpose is to identify what's going on in the marketplace and show how some organizations are harnessing some of the macro trends to be more competitive. I'm simply saying, in this instance, with this particular idea or innovation, this organization has done some specific thing that we would all be wise to go to school on. The specific details of these organizations are not particularly important to the purpose of this discussion.

By providing some examples of the thought process behind harnessing some of these trends in a variety of settings, it will help trigger thoughts that can prove helpful to you in applying some of these things to your situation in your current organization.

First, let me share a couple of observations from my years of working with organizations.

There are two big myths I believe inhibit a lot of organizations ability to thrive in their specific marketplace.

The first myth is recognizing that just about any organization, of any size, in any marketplace, can harness these trend insights to create a greater measure of success. A disproportionate degree of success is more about courage than it is about capability.

You don't need to have an in-house Mensa Club to become more successful than most others in your marketplace. Moving forward and standing out distinctively has more to do with the courage to innovate, to try different things, to think differently, to behave distinctively than it does about any innate, collective, technical capability inside an organization.

Any organization, or component part of an organization, can harness these trends to make itself more successful, or at the very least, to make the environment a more stimulating, more fun, and more satisfying place to work.

The second myth has to do with brilliant new ideas.

Many of us spend a lot of time looking for the grand, game-changing, revolutionary, brilliant idea that will instantly leapfrog us many multiples ahead of our competitors.

I am certainly not against brilliant, breakthrough ideas. If you have the capacity to conceive of the next Google, or iPod, or Facebook, congratulations – that will be a wonderful thing. However, the vast majority of organizations are not going to conceive and execute that kind of industry-changing, brilliant idea. I tell my clients, that achieving more than their fair share of success in their marketplace has much less to do with looking for brilliant new ideas, than it does with the disciplined execution of good ideas.

Virtually every organization I've ever worked with has filing drawers full of good ideas. These are the little, incremental changes and improvements that can be made to systems, procedures, communications, products, and services. I've also learned that many, many, many of these ideas never get beyond a flip chart in the meeting room, or the file notes inside that cabinet drawer. Successful organizations are those that have implemented mechanisms giving them the ability to put many more of these ideas into practice than a typical organization does.

It is the disciplined execution of good ideas over a period of time that cumulatively creates substantial, competitive advantage. Brilliant new ideas are a great thing if you happen to come across them, but the disciplined execution of good ideas is available to everyone. That is a much surer route to success for the vast majority of organizations.

Inside the Box

One of the most hackneyed phrases in business over the last several years has been, "think outside the box". This implies an ability to think in innovative, brand new ways.

It is my observation that many organizations can benefit tremendously from spending a little more time, thinking a little more deeply 'inside the box'. They need to focus on the things they are already doing and determine how to do them better; not only better than they are currently doing them, but better than anyone else is doing them!

It's fine to have brand new, creative perspectives on other things that we could be doing, or brand-spanking new ways to approach some of the things we are doing. Yet, many of us can enhance the value of our offerings to the world, if we worry less about thinking 'outside the box' and spend more time thinking 'inside the box' about the ways we can improve what we are already doing.

As you read through some of these various trends, think about how they can apply, even in small ways, to improve what is actually going on, right now, inside your 25 square feet of the universe, in your current organization.

Another Toronto boy named Marshall McLuhan (he of the *global village* and *electronic fireplace*) had a wonderful expression. He said, "I wouldn't have seen it if I hadn't believed it."

One of the things that will happen from my sharing some of these trends, is you're going to drive around your familiar territory, you're going to look at some of the things you have looked at before, but you are going to see something different.

Why will this happen? Having this new or expanded information may result in giving the kaleidoscope of your mind a twist, creating a slightly different picture or a different lens through which you can observe what's happening.

Trends Are Interrelated

You'll see as we look at these trends that they are interrelated. Organizations that are thriving and those getting ready to leapfrog their competition are those that, in the current vernacular, are 'firing on all cylinders'.

Some of the examples could easily fit under two or three different headings. I've divided the trends into headings, making them easier to understand and to integrate into everyday thinking. However, many of them really represent several trends, harnessed simultaneously, creating innovations in products or marketing or operations. The key is to grab the ones that provide some insight for you – understanding how they will positively impact some of the things you are doing – inside your organization.

Technology Creates Transparency

Let's start with the trend that isn't – technology!

Technology unto itself is not a trend; it is a tool. It is something we use to capture and harness some of the trends we see going on around us, in the way we go about delivering and creating products and services. It certainly accelerates and facilitates some trends; it slows down and hampers others. But unto itself, technology is just a tool; it's not a specific trend.

We talked earlier about the big impact of technology in the latter part of the 20th and early 21st centuries, leveling the playing field and facilitating the explosion in micro-business and the transition into the knowledge-based economy. What we're seeing now is *technology creating transparency.*

This means that how we operate as an organization, the decision making processes that go on internally, and the end result for those who deal with us, are visible, or can certainly become visible, to anyone who wants to know.

If mission and value statements are supposed to provide behavior and decision making guidance to the troops in an organization, perhaps, it was an intuitive understanding of this macro trend that led Google to infamously have as its overriding mission to "Do no evil".

Much of our earlier discussion can be summed up as devolution of power. We have moved from an age where almost all power in every sector was tightly concentrated, with a relatively tiny number of people, to a universe where much more power is disseminated much more broadly, across many more people.

Mark Twain famously observed, "One should never pick a fight with a man who buys his ink by the barrel." He was referring to the power of the media to disseminate information.

While it is still true that major news sources and media outlets have great influence on what we see and read and know, it is also true that we are seeing an unprecedented explosion in the number of sources available for finding information on a virtually limitless number of topics.

The closest parallel to what we are witnessing now, would probably be the first translations of the Bible into English in Western Europe several hundreds years ago, which caused massive social upheaval.

This trend of *technology creating transparency* is showing up all over the place, when we recognize it for what it is. Some of these have serious implications, both socially, and for our business organizations; some are just interesting, and some are just fun!

One of my favorite examples is a website called GetHuman.com. The website says (June 2009):

> "The gethuman™ movement has been created from the voices of millions of consumers who want to be treated with dignity when they contact a company for customer support."

This is a free website, also available through an iPhone app, run by volunteers, and it boasts over a million users. It pools the collective experience of many thousands of people to address one of the common frustrations regularly experienced by most of the citizens of the developed world: phoning an 800 number for tech support, customer service, etc. knowing full well, before making the call, you will be plunged into 'phone tree hell'.

You know the drill – please punch in your 16-digit number, please punch in your mother's birthday, please punch in the address of the first school you went to, please punch in . . . . etc. etc. etc.

Have you ever noticed that most of these robotic questions start off with the advisory, "Please listen carefully because our options have recently changed."

No matter where I've been lately, on several continents and in a dozen countries, an interesting phenomenon is happening –

apparently "the options have recently changed" in every business all over the world! What a coincidence?!

Around the world, there are very large organizations, which have invested huge amounts of money, in very sophisticated software; it's all fundamentally designed to make sure no one ever gets to interrupt any of their people while they're at work.

What Get Human has done is posted a thousand or more of these 800 numbers, organized by industry and company name. They also posted the sequence of buttons you can punch to go around each organization's phone tree and get to a real, live human being.

On a connected site, Get2Human.com, you can rank the quality of the service you received when you eventually reached a person. A twist on this site includes giving you an opportunity to comment on how <u>understandable</u> the person on the other end of the phone was when you spoke with them. This, is in reaction to all the outsourcing to various call centers around the world – you can rank from 1-5 Red Flags, based on how difficult it was to understand the person on the other end of the phone.

A large bank in the UK has a note on this site beside their customer service line that says, "Just keep hitting 0 when it asks for your 16-digit account number; then press 2 to go directly to an account manager." This is probably a result from the frequent customer frustration from punching in all this information into the phone. Adding insult to injury, when you finally get to talk with the person on the other end, you have to repeat it all again because you discover they don't have any of the information on the screen in front of them.

One of the telephone companies in Canada invested an enormous amount of money in a voice-activated, virtual person named Emily, to guide phone calls. The note beside their number gives you some buttons to push and in brackets says, "Ignore Emily."

What we have, then, is the collective experience and frustration of the crowd, easily defeating the software design and investment of these large organizations.

There are now lots of websites that give people an opportunity to report on their experiences with the hospitality industry. One of them, holidays-uncovered.co.uk, has 50 thousand reports on various holiday package tours all over the world. These are unadulterated, direct reports of individual customer experiences. It is getting harder and harder to promise one thing in the brochure and deliver something else on the ground with impunity.

Another UK website, mysupermarket.co.uk, allows you to collect a shopping cart full of groceries and automatically compare the price of those groceries at four major supermarkets. You can also send the order for that cart of groceries to the store of your choice. This is dramatically changing the old loss leader/bait and switch strategy of the weekly flyer.

We are seeing similar things in other sectors. There are more and more sites that allow consumers to research and compare the track records of healthcare providers, for instance, in many countries.

Ratemyteachers.com claims 10 million listings, across several countries. This is a site causing all sorts of ripples and various reactions from students, parents, school administrators, teachers and their union. Once again, *technology is creating* (a level of) *transparency* these constituencies must adapt to quickly.

Planningalerts.com takes advantage of the digitization of some functions of local government. All submissions to the planning department, for changes of any kind in a community, have gone digital. This site allows residents to sign up to be automatically advised of any submission to the planning department affecting property within an extremely specific geographic area.

If someone is planning to build a big garage on the side of a property, all the neighbors will know about it the minute the application is submitted to the local planning authority.

On a broader scale, we see an interesting phenomenon that started in China and is now being picked up in California (in fact, the most interesting part of this trend may be that it started in China and then migrated to California). It is sometimes referred to as 'tuangou'. In China individuals were using the Internet and their cell phones to form themselves into spontaneous buying groups. The term 'tuangou' roughly means 'gang buying'.

The scenario: someone sends out a message saying he wants to buy model XYZ washing machine. Who else wants to buy the same machine?

In the beginning they arranged to physically meet in the parking lot of an appliance store, one person went into the store, found the manager and said, "I'm interested in buying model XYZ washing machine, and in the parking lot are 247 of my friends who want to buy exactly the same machine. What is the price now?"

In Canada, recently, a preeminent lawyer and political figure was appointed to chair a Royal Commission investigating a social issue. He quickly found himself the subject of a page on a social networking site. Individual citizens, across the country, were using the site to coordinate and plan appearances before the Commission. They were also providing responses and submissions on the subject he was investigating.

This transparency phenomenon is affecting not only large entities in the public and private sectors, but individuals as well.

A dating site, dontdatehimgirl.com, is pretty much what you would expect it to be, based on its URL. It allows searches by individual names, and numerous entries begin, "This guy is my ex-fiancé . . ."

Every initiative that creates a problem gives birth to the opportunity for solution. If you choose to investigate the above site, you should also check out defendmyname.com, which does pretty much what you would expect it to do, based on its URL.

Smart recruiters looking to hire fresh graduates are now making a point of checking MySpace, Facebook, and the like, before making a final offer to a job applicant.

Perhaps one of the most useful sites is Google Alerts. This site allows you to type in a name or term and ask Google to troll the net every few hours or days and send you a link to everywhere the term or name has appeared on the net within that time frame. Switched on individuals are using it beyond their names, or their organizations names, to also put themselves in the 'first to know' category for news about key clients, or suppliers, or competitors, or targeted prospects with whom they want to do business. Google Alerts has the added benefit of being free.

We could spend several hundred pages talking about the technologies that are going to create solutions to many of our overriding problems – solutions in many fields, from medicine, to food production, to energy, and to the environment. We know technology is constantly changing the way we work and communicate, as well as the way many organizations market and communicate with their customers and clients. But the macro trend that is surging along below the surface is the way *technology is creating transparency* in every element of everything we do.

Personality *is* the Brand

I believe organizations, or divisions, or departments, or branches develop personalities just like people do. In my own experience, listening to the way individuals talk about suppliers, or customers, or other divisions within an organization, the words used to describe them are the same words used to describe people.

One may be talking about a client organization and comment, "They are great people to deal with." They are easy going, or cooperative, or helpful, or very professional, or quite thorough, or fun to deal with; on the other hand, another organization might be described as aggressive, condescending, difficult, unethical, nit-picking, or humorless.

This is remarkable if you think about it. Often an organization represents hundreds, if not thousands, of people and yet it is described as if it were an individual. I believe all organizations have personalities. What is happening now is that the *personality* – what they are actually like to deal with, on a day-to-day basis – *is*, de facto becoming *the brand*.

It doesn't matter, what advertising, or public relations, or corporate communications may say. What an organization is really like to deal with, decision-by-decision, interaction-by-interaction, day-in and day-out – in other words the *personality* of the unit is becoming the brand!

I tell executives there are four things they need to understand about branding in today's environment.

1. You don't own your brand.
2. The conversation in the marketplace owns your brand.
3. You cannot control that conversation.
4. You can only participate in the conversation.

This has always been true, to some degree. What is happening now is that the conversation is so widespread and happens so quickly, that it is much, much truer today than it has ever been.

When that conversation, in what I call the 'omniblog' – all the various ezines, blogs, networking sites, bulletin boards, twitterings, etc. – reaches any kind of consensus, it defines your brand for your marketplace. The challenge for organizations is to locate and then participate in these conversations.

Leading organizations today have people whose purpose is to monitor that conversation in the 'omniblog', and then contribute to it, or disseminate it internally for others to act on. This allows them to be aware of what the market is saying and gives them an opportunity to influence - not control – how conversation evolves.

To some, on first glance, this will look like another one of those 'airy-fairy, fuzzy, consultant-theory-type' things. It is not. This is a serious, hard business reality in today's marketplace.

A few years ago, a major computer manufacturer decided to cut costs by cutting, and outsourcing much of their tech-support, thereby tangibly reducing the availability of personnel to respond to customer enquiries. In short order, a couple of influential bloggers started writing about this change in their strategy, or at least the visible change in the way they were doing business.

Within a few months, the tom-toms beating out in cyberspace created a major customer backlash that was eventually picked up by mainstream media. The end result: their stock price was hammered by over 20%; they were forced to take dramatic action after all the appropriate 'mea culpa's'. The point: they did not pick up this brewing grass fire quickly enough to respond before it became such a major conflagration.

Many executives might struggle with the concept of defining *'personality'* to the marketplace, but none of them have any difficulty understanding "the stock dropped 20%."

I first met Steve Ballmer (at an event in Fargo, of all places) when he was the Chief Operating Officer of Microsoft. During our conversation, he told me that his number one strategic priority, at that time, was to get the various parts of Microsoft working more effectively together. Sometime later, when he became Chief Executive Officer of Microsoft, he said "My number one strategic priority as CEO is to redefine and reshape the *personality* of Microsoft as an organization." (His words; not mine).

We later saw Microsoft settling numerous legal actions, releasing some of its source code, and striking a variety of different kinds of 'partnership' arrangements with several competitors. This was the tactical manifestation of that strategic priority in action.

If acting on this *personality is the brand* concept can become the strategic executive priority at Microsoft, it is probably something worth considering for leadership at all levels in any organization.

Another well-known organization, that has taken personality branding to the extreme, is the Virgin group of companies, headed by Richard Branson. Some may argue that Branson and his Virgin corporation have become as much a branding machine as an operating company. The Virgin logo is on a tremendously diverse series of businesses around the world, from bookstores to airlines, to soda pop, to health club services, to mobile phone services, to Internet services. Just about the only thing this collection of businesses has in common is the Virgin label.

The remarkable thing to me is the consistency with which these businesses have adopted the *personality branding* philosophy. Whether you're dealing with the health club in South Africa, or the mobile phone service in Australia, or the retail store in Toronto, they have a philosophy of doing business and an attitude toward life that is remarkably similar across all these companies.

How does an organization's personality show through? Some time back, I was in Coolangotta Airport in Australia, catching a Virgin Blue Airline flight to Sydney. After going through all the security procedures, I stopped and took some photographs of one of the familiar sites in any airport, the carryon luggage-sizing device. Almost everywhere around the world, huge signs full of warnings and diagrams about weight and dimensions sit atop these things.

The Virgin Blue station had three different carryon sizing-devices, also with great big signs. The first one said, "You can have a huge ego, but only a bag this size."

The next one said, "All the emotional baggage you want, as long as it fits in here."

The third one, in great big letters, simply said, "Size really does matter."

That is a great example of an organization exhibiting parts of its personality that differentiates it from everyone else.

Here's the leadership lesson for everyone who influences the way an organization exhibits its personality. I'm pretty sure that Richard Branson did not get into one of his planes and fly to Coolangatta Airport in Australia and write the script for the carryon luggage-sizers. Yet, the staff at Virgin Blue obviously "gets it". They understand what the company is about and the personality they are trying to project to their customers.

Another great example of an airline with a very distinctive personality is Southwest Airlines in the United States. Casual uniforms, humorous cabin announcements, and an almost party-like atmosphere are trademarks of every flight (along with the ubiquitous peanuts).

The fundamental role of leadership has become: to define the personality they want their organization exhibiting, and then get that personality well enough understood inside, that it is consistently visible outside. (Most MBA courses don't teach that.)

Here are some other organizations letting their personalities show:

- Coast Capital Savings Credit Union's (British Columbia, Canada) website has a link represented by a picture of a cell phone; on the cell phone is this message: "Hw cn we hlp u?:)" ('How can we help you?' in Twitter-script). The portion of their website that lists their executives and board of directors has a line under the link that says, "They're not just a bunch of pretty faces; check out some of their pretty faces here." This gives a sense of what kind of financial institution they would be to deal with.

- The Mortgage and Finance Association of Australia has a whole series of questions and answers on the FAQs section of their website. One example: "If I need help buying a home, what should I do?" The answer: "Be nice to your parents." A link is provided for help with multi-generational household financing.

- A roadhouse-style restaurant's opening announcement says "Yes, We Are Now Open" Under this headline, a textbox says, "We've got the building permit, the gas permit, the liquor permit, the restaurant permit, the health permit, and the permit to have all these permits."

- Emirates Airlines is working to position itself as a global airline. Its' ad campaign is touting one of the significant differences it has made to achieve this goal. Almost all airlines staff their planes with their own nationals. (As an example, the 'Singapore Airlines girl' has become an icon in the travel business). The Emirates ads brag that their staff represents 90 different nationalities.

- The incredibly successful series of television ads Apple has been running around the world – "Hello I'm a PC; Hello I'm a Mac" theme, is another great example of personality branding at work.

- The Faith Community United Credit Union, originally serving members of Mt. Sinai Baptist Church, is located in one of the decidedly less prosperous neighborhoods of Cleveland, Ohio. Under the leadership of CEO Rita Haynes, it offers special products like the 'Mercy Mortgage Bailout' loan. It also provides 'Grace' loans, small, short-term loans, allowing members to establish a payback history, which then qualifies them to apply for longer-term 'Amazing Grace' loans. Those who develop a longer, better credit history then qualify for a 'Greater

Grace' line of credit. This type of very targeted, personality branding has helped to triple their membership over the last several years. As an interesting aside, 75% of the borrowers have been bankrupt, yet the delinquency rates are less than 0.1%, a rate most big banks would kill for.

Speaking of large financial institutions, next is one working to change the stereotype personality of these organizations.

- Capital One's website says, as a preface to it's agreement button for all the legalities required, "First things first: sorry to start out with the legal stuff, but we'll need you to read these terms and conditions and agree to them by clicking the check-box before you can use online banking."

- Even TSA, the organization responsible for all airport security screenings in the United States, is showing signs of putting a practical, helpful face on doing its job. In the airport in Charlotte, North Carolina, at the entrance area of the great, winding maze of crowd control pylons and ropes is a sign guiding people to three separate entrances. It's done in the color and shapes of the signs on ski hills indicating the level of difficulty of various runs. Beside the green circle it says, 'Family Lane', beside the blue box it says, 'Casual Traveler', and beside the black diamond it says, 'Expert Traveler'.

The headline at the top says, "Help us help you. What kind of traveler are you?" Seems to be a rather personable and practical initiative to me. My question is, "With the amount of traveling I do, why this is the only time I've ever seen this?"

Very small businesses have the luxury of letting their personalities, and sense of humor, show if they feel so inclined.

- When the gas prices spiked in 2008, one gas station posted a sign board for the three grades of gasoline that read: 'Arm', 'Leg', and 'First Born'.

- During our last election campaign, I drove by a truck that pumps out septic tanks. On the back was a sign that said "Warning; may be carrying political promises."

It made me smile. When's the last time your organization did something that made everyone smile?

Micro-marketing

The *micro-marketing* trend is all about making small differences in the products and services an organization provides to make them more appealing, more easily usable, or a more precise fit for specific elements of the customer base. Success in today's market environment is very much about figuring out ways to be something very special to someone in particular.

The days of the large, broad, appeal-to-everyone organizations are gone. The mass market that these organizations served has disappeared. The large, old-line department stores/general merchandisers that sold just about everything to the 'common consumer' slowly saw every element of their marketplace stolen by providers specializing in specific market segments.

The likes of Home Depot, Toys R Us, Best Buy, Foot Locker, etc. each took a chunk of their customers. Those that have survived have radically changed the line of merchandise they carry to be much more focused, and to be seen as specializing in certain areas.

The need to do this was driven by the disappearance of the mass market, as consumers demanded more and more options and specialization in everything they wanted to buy.

The same thing has happened in every marketplace and every element of business. One of the reasons so many large organizations struggle with the concept of the *personality is the brand* trend, is their tradition of wanting to be 'all things to all people'. In that environment, the priority became not to offend anyone. Therefore, we ended up with huge organizations that quite consciously had hammered all the personality out of every element of their organizations. We ended up with massive, bland, faceless institutions.

A great example of what an organization was and what one can become is IBM – having successfully reinvented itself more than once. In the 1960's the 'uniform' at IBM was a white shirt, tie, and a dark suit. Wearing a light blue shirt was considered a radical, career-limiting statement of individuality. Today, IBMers only wear 'business dress' when a specific customer expects it. And IBM sells highly customized services, not one-size-fits-all hardware.

All organizations need to figure out ways to identify and appeal to specific segments of their customer base. *Micro-marketing* is one of the ways smart organizations are doing it.

A great example of the power of *micro-marketing* is the book *Chicken Soup for the Teenage Soul*. This book sold 3,000,000 more copies in one year than the original *Chicken Soup for the Soul*, sold in three years. And look at the title selection now!

Here are some ways a variety of organizations are harnessing this idea of *micro-marketing*:

- In India, a motor scooter manufacturer wants to sell more scooters to women. How do you make something like a motor scooter a 'woman's' product? The solution, apparently, is to put a special little hook on the column, under the seat, designed to hold a handbag. This tiny change to the product solves a very real problem for that particular customer group.

- In Australia there is a magazine called *iLove*, specifically targeted to women commuters. It's a 32-page, glossy magazine that covers the gamut of topics found in most women's general interest magazines. It's a little bit smaller than *Reader's Digest*-size, but it comes attached as a label on a bottle of water! *iLove* produces a new issue approximately every ten days, and is now the number one magazine in Australia, the most competitive magazine market in the world.

The young woman who came up with this idea patented the technology that makes it possible, calling it 'On Product Publishing'. She did her first big deal with Coca Cola in Belgium, and it's now being used in a variety of ways, including a cooking magazine on bread packaging, and a pregnancy magazine on vitamin packaging. She's recently done a deal with Tetrapak to do 'on product publishing' for its wide variety of products.

- Also from Australia comes the 'Burqini', a swimsuit specifically designed for conservative Muslim women. It is made of light fabrics, allowing these young women to enjoy the water comfortably, while maintaining the modesty they want. These are sold all over the world. When speaking at a leadership event in Bahrain recently, I used this particular item as an innovation example. All around the conference hall, heads nodded in recognition. Everyone in the room knew someone who owned one. I couldn't help but ask this audience, "Where were the local innovators when this particular product was being developed? Why is something like this *Australian*?"

- In Dubai, Moscow, and London there are taxi services specifically targeting women as customers. They provide an assurance of safe, clean, and polite services that are particularly appealing to that market segment. In Mexico City, for many of the same reasons, there is a bus service available exclusively for women.

- *Wedvert* is a magazine for brides and grooms who want to have an eco-friendly wedding. It's especially interesting to see this type of targeted magazine, and there are thousands of equally targeted magazines, when you remember that the conventional wisdom 20 years ago was that the Internet would kill the magazine business (just as it was assumed that the advent of television would kill all radio). Today there are more magazine titles than ever.

■ Coast Capital Savings Credit Union (still located in British Columbia, Canada) ran a campaign called "I Love Fees", which was an entire tongue-in-cheek exercise poking fun at the big banks in Canada for all the fees the banks charge. Each branch displayed a gigantic 'thank you card' for its members to sign. A series of TV ads showed people talking about why they *love* big bank fees. These ads are on their website for people to enjoy again, and send the link to their friends. The *micro-marketing* element: these ads are also available in Punjabi, Cantonese, and Mandarin, which makes a lot of sense if you're doing business in Vancouver.

■ An Australian mortgage broker specializes in gay-friendly home loans. What a great example of how you can take something like cash, the ultimate commodity, and *micro-market* by addressing the needs of a specific marketplace.

■ In England, Sheila's Wheels sells home and car insurance – pretty generic products. Their research said the typical woman in England has £285 of contents in her purse. The standard clause in insurance policies has a limit of £85 of coverage for the loss of a purse. They changed their policy to provide coverage for up to £300. Their home insurance includes unlimited coverage for shoes, make-up, handbags, and clothing. They also created a list of female-friendly car repair shops for their customers. In the insurance business, the claims difference between £85 and £300 coverage for a purse is negligible, as is the extra coverage for shoes or make-up. By making minor changes to their product, they created a very special appeal to that particular market.

What we see is a wide variety of organizations adapting this micro-marketing trend to their individual situations, and reaping the rewards inherent in this approach.

Now that you're aware of it, you'll no doubt recognize lots more of it in the weeks and months ahead.

The Next Service Revolution: Customer Intelligence

No, this is not the never-ending search for smarter customers; this is about how we use the intelligence we already have about our customers.

Leading organizations are aggressively harnessing the increasingly inexpensive data-crunching capability that exists today, to mine for additional insights about their customers. They are also using a wide variety of other mechanisms to better crawl inside their customers' heads and better understand how they think. The better an organization understands its customers and the issues and challenges they face, the better that organization can create solutions of particular appeal to them.

Often when I introduce this subject, the knee-jerk reaction I get is "Oh, we're already on that. We do customer satisfaction surveys all the time."

Well, good. And so you should. But that has nothing to do with what I'm talking about here.

There are two kinds of customer information a smart organization wants to have.

One is benchmarks for consistency. This is the stuff customer satisfaction surveys deliver. The focus is measurement against set standards for a variety of specific criteria. (How long did you wait on hold; did your server recommend a desert; did your shipment arrive complete and on time; would you recommend us to your friends?). You need this information to measure existing performance, and track internal trends. But it's maintenance.

It will not help you create a better product, deliver a different service, or build a better company.

The second kind of information that is powerful is insight for enhancement. This is beyond, 'How well are we doing what we do now?' It's even beyond, 'What else should we be doing?'

This is, 'Let me understand you and your world, and then I'll figure out what I can do to make it better for you.'

This concept was well captured on a broad, corporate level by Akio Morita, as he built Sony into a world leader in its field.

He said, "Our plan is to lead the public with new products rather than ask them what they want. The public does not know what is possible, but we do."

Hal Sperlich, (father of the minivan) says: "In ten years of developing the minivan, not once did we get a letter from a housewife asking us to invent one." (This evidence of no-demand-for-it kept Henry Ford from approving the concept. It came to fruition when Sperlich and Lee Iacocca were at Chrysler as it was teetering on bankruptcy, around 1980, and had nothing to lose.)

There are a myriad of ways to collect these insights into how people actually use products and services, and the issues they face in the relevant parts of their lives. (Proctor & Gamble does 'immersion research', having researchers in peoples homes for hours, watching them cook, clean, and change the baby!)

But you don't need to go to those kinds of extremes to become part of the *next service revolution*. You can use the information you already have available, or perhaps turn the data you have into useful information, to look for opportunities.

Almost every organization has more information available about its customers than it is effectively using. *Customer Intelligence* is about finding ways to harness the insights in that information to figure out ways to better serve those customers and enhance your business.

Best Buy, the giant appliances and electronics retailer, is a smart company.

They crunched sales data from 60 million transactions, trying to find out how the old 80/20 rule applied to them (80% of your profits come form 20% of your customers). What they discovered in their stores was that 100% of their profits came from 20% of their customers!

These are obviously very rounded numbers, but equally obviously, some of their customers were a lot more valuable than others.

They undertook an initiative they called Customer Centricity in a couple of dozen stores.

In an effort to turn more customers into high-margin buyers, they invested very big dollars in intensive training programs for several categories of merchandise. Then when someone came into a store interested in one of those categories, they'd be introduced to a staff member who had been through that specific training. Audiophiles, photographers, small business owners, and each was able to deal with staff with very extensive knowledge of their needs, and the product line.

Sales went up 100%. Color this one successful.

In 2008 they opened a new pilot store in Denver based on another insight. Despite being traditionally seen as a guys gadget store, they determined that 45% of the buying decisions in their stores were being made by women. So they convened a panel of 40 women, and said, "You know our product line. If you were running this store as a place you'd like to shop, what would it look like?"

It does not look like a normal Best Buy store. There are room groupings as displays. The 'Home Theatre' section is called 'Family Room'. The details don't matter, and we'll see how this pilot evolves, but it is indicative of the way they go about constantly working to innovate to stay ahead of their competitors. All of it originating by looking at their own data.

It's been pretty effective. One of their largest competitors, Circuit City, went into liquidation in early 2009.

In the UK, Tesco, primarily a grocery retailer, crunches 12 billion transactions from 12 million card holders, and sends out 6 million different letters every quarter highlighting products and services it knows are of interest to that particular customer. It now offers a host of peripheral convenience services in addition to groceries.

It is this kind of thinking that has taken them form the number three retailer in England, to the number three retailer in the world.

Recently I got a glossy brochure in the mail from Chapters, a large Canadian bookseller. I'm a reader; I have their frequent shopper card. The front of this brochure said "Dear Warren Evans, these spring titles have been selected based on your purchase history."

I don't know how many variations of this brochure they printed, but about five times as many titles in that brochure piqued my interest compared to any of their previous, generic mail-outs.

Earlier this year a woman who runs a home and auto insurance company in Australia was telling me a great story about really knowing your customer.

They had been aggressively going after the young drivers and first time home buyers in their market. They invested in a website that could deliver comparisons and quotes, and actual policies if people chose to buy. This was intended to be a big cost saver that would help lower premiums for this market segment.

Their website was busy, yet only 10% of those that received a quote, and started filling out the application, actually bought online. They also knew that 80% of those buying in an office had been quoted online. Marketing decided this proved that even the younger generation was uncomfortable buying insurance online.

This made no sense to the CEO. This group buys everything online. Why not their insurance? Scrambling for answers, she gathered a group of 20-somethings from around the office, and asked them if they could explain what was happening.

They appeared surprised that she did not know! They assumed it was an executive decision, although it made no sense to them.

Near the end of the online application was a box for a phone number. The site's software then automatically interfaced with the telephone company's database to verify the phone number against the address entered. If it didn't match, the site tossed the application out. There is a kind of logic at work here.

A large percentage of this demographic does not own a landline phone. Their mobile phones are all they have. They wanted to buy online, but the site wouldn't let them. The most faithful among them made the trek to an office.

Had they looked further into the data, marketing could have known the exact spot people bailed off the site.

If some of that young office staff had spoken up, they would have known a lot faster. In smart organizations, customer intelligence is everybody's business!

On a personal level, when you are given a project, it is less important for you to understand what it is someone says they want, than for you to understand what it is they want it _for_. If you understand the problem they are trying to solve, or the solution they are asking you to create, you can put all your knowledge and resources to work and provide them with the most effective end-result.

Henry Ford (the original) is reported to have said, "If I'd asked people what they wanted, they would have told me 'a faster horse'."

Yesterday, in the days of the mass market, we kept our customers because they knew us. Tomorrow, in the age of micro-marketing, we will keep them because *we* know *them*.

Simplification Gets HOT!

Simplification focuses on making the customer's life simpler, rather than more complicated. The complexity of virtually every element of life has increased exponentially over the last several years. It is extremely true in the technology arena. That's why the vast majority of people only use about 10% of the capability of most of the technology they own.

When I have a new device, from a Blackberry to a television remote control, my challenge is to try and identify the three buttons, out of all those available, that will actually perform the three or four functions that I bought the thing to do.

Helping children decide what courses they should take in school used to be a relatively simple exercise. Now it requires the skills of an investigative journalist just to make a reasonably educated 'guess' as to what might be most appropriate.

In this world of increasing complexity anyone who can simplify the process of doing business with them wins not only my loyalty, but my love!

One of the most successful magazine launches in the last decade was *Real Simple*, a magazine dedicated to helping people simplify every aspect of life – home, food, money, health, work, and family. Hugely successful, *Real Simple* is about nothing except how to make everything else simpler!

A sommelier in New York City believed passionately that pairing the right wine with the right food mattered a great deal. He recognized that lots of people don't do it because it's too difficult. He created a line of wines, using the labels on the bottles to indicate which food goes with this wine, to simplify the process. The wine that goes best with fish has a picture of a fish on the label; the wine that goes with chicken has a picture of a chicken on the label; the wine for beef has a steak. He even has one with a pizza on the label. It is a most successful initiative!

The stunning success of the Flip video camera is amazing. This small, super simple video recorder has a USB plug built-in. When the device is plugged into a computer, a menu pops up asking, "Do you want to upload this to a website? Save it to a file? Send it to someone?" An incredibly simple device to use in a market full of stunningly complicated devices.

A cell phone provider put out a brochure touting eight of their available cell phones. Instead of detailing all the technical specifications and capabilities for each phone, the headlines focused on the appropriate user for each phone: 'Super Mom'; the 'Recent Grad'; 'Movers and Shakers'; 'Gadget Freaks'; 'Social Butterflies'; 'Outdoor Lovers'. The phones are basically the same product. But by identifying an appropriate user, the potential customer is saved from doing technical comparisons. It simplifies the buying process, especially for gift givers.

Not everyone who can benefit from having a cell phone needs or wants to make movies, surf the Internet, or play games – they simply want to be able to make and receive phone calls.

Samsung's Jitterbug, released in the latter half of 2008, is designed for those who may be uncomfortable with electronic gadgetry. A simple keypad, large buttons, and large type size on the screen provide the basics. When ordering, you can send in the names and numbers you want in your contacts list, and the phone comes to you preloaded with your request.

The super-simple version has only three buttons on the front – one says 'operator', another 'tow', and the third '911'. Will it succeed? The jury is still out, but Samsung's research indicates there is a need for a product this simple.

Simplification is not just about simplifying products and services. It's also about simplifying the internal processes in organizations to provide more streamlined and simplified interfaces to the outside world.

GE Money's Merchant Enrollment mechanism is an interesting case study. Although GE Money has chosen to withdraw from some markets, its example of the possible is still instructive.

GE Money is a service providing retailers with the ability to offer financing of purchases to their customers. When you go into your local, independent jewelry store, and purchase some jewelry by financing it for a year, the store is not doing the financing; GE Money is the organization behind the retailer that is providing the financing. By going on a campaign to simplify the process for merchants to sign up to do business, they increased market share dramatically.

At the start, it took 63 days from the time a merchant signed on for the service to the time that store could offer financing to its customers. By re-thinking their internal processes, GE Money was able to cut this time period from 63 days to 1 day! (No, that's not a typo. They went from 63 days to one!) The resulting campaign was called "Enroll Today – Transact Tomorrow" and it's not surprising that sales increased by 100% using the revised, simplified process.

If an organization as large and complex as GE can take a process that entailed extending credit through a second party, and simplify it from 63 days to one, we should all be inspired to revisit all the functions within our organizations for potential *simplification*.

I tell leadership and management audiences that if they don't know how to start this process, they should ask the staff what they hate.

Almost always, the things that staff hates dealing with are the same things the customers hate. It won't do the job of taking full advantage of the idea, but it's certainly a great place to start.

In every organization I've worked with, there have always been dozens of things to do to simplify and streamline processes. Cumulatively they have a huge impact on what it is like for the customer to deal with the organization.

This trend is also very true, inside our organizations, as various functions deal with each other as internal customers.

Almost every form of business has some sort of legal disclaimers, instructions, limits, etc. that must be part of the information it provides to its customers. It's a great education to see the variety of ways this information can be presented.

A favorite of mine is to look at the difference in the verbiage on airline e-tickets. Most of us print out the confirmation, keep the front page that has the flight numbers and departure times, and throw out the other four pages of 'legalese'. Read that 'stuff' one day, compare how most of the newer, low-cost carriers present it, with how the traditional, old-line carriers deliver what is basically the same information.

The benchmark opportunity is to read *your* 'stuff'. What does the peripheral information, coming from your department, division, or company actually say? How does it feel to an outsider reading it for the first time? Does it appear to assume higher intelligence? Is it cooperative, friendly, conversational, and straightforward, or is it arrogant, condescending, demanding, aggressive, or even obnoxious? Is it simple to understand and reasonable to agree with, or does it come across as complex and intimidating?

No one wrote this 'stuff' to be offensive to others (unless, of course someone let 'legal' near the customer interface point, which is seldom a good idea). Yet, these things just seem to grow over time into this type of format, and in most organizations, are rarely read to see what is actually being distributed to the customers.

One benchmark to check all of this against, one of the Gold Standards, is Skype. It's a great example of how *personality* and *simplification* have come together to create an ultimate, customer-friendly experience. The technology and what is does is valuable and compelling. This combination of *personality branding* and *simplification* is one of the big reasons Skype went from a few dozen users to 200 million downloads with virtually no advertising budget at all. Check it out at skype.com.

Check your organization's *simplification*-focus by clicking on whatever button on your website is there to allow visitors to communicate with the organization. Does it open up your email browser to send an email, or does it open up an online form with a series of boxes that must be filled in to submit a request? Perform the same experiment on the media area of your site.

For me wanting to communicate with you, filling out a form to submit a comment or question feels like submitting an application, so that you can determine if I am worthy of your attention. It also eats up my time. These forms often include fields which can't possibly be relevant to crossing the 'acceptable to communicate with' threshold. And if your form won't take my postal code, I can't communicate with you. Brilliant.

Something that consistently amazes me: the reason there is a media section on any organization's website, is to give the organization a fighting chance of participating in any conversations going on about the organization. Speed is the lifeblood of media. I want a chance to talk to any of the media before they go to air or to print with something that involves my organization. How I choose to handle the connection is up to me, but I always want it to be my decision.

Surveys tell us that when media people hit one of these 'fill out the form' pages instead of a direct e-mail, 97% of them simply bounce off the page and go somewhere else. Almost all of them! The primary purpose of having a media page is defeated by the complexity of this 'little thing'. Where they'll go instead, we can't know. What we do know is the organization has lost the opportunity to have a first 'kick at the can' with that story.

Generally speaking these things exist, not from any managerial or strategic decision, but because someone, somewhere in the web design corner of the organization, has simply cut and pasted a form from somewhere else.

I'm flattered to be asked to speak at numerous conferences and management meetings. Several years ago I decided to see if I could simplify this speaking part of my business for our clients. It was already a simple, model: a client paid my fee, and after the event I invoiced them for travel and related expenses. Everyone worked this way; clients expected it – that's just the way it was.

But it did have some parts that everybody hated, mostly the chasing around of taxi receipts and other small expenses.

So I changed the model. My fees now include all travel and miscellaneous expenses. My clients love it because they know exactly what their total cost will be in advance, and they have no paperwork to do after the fact.

I lose a bit on the apples and win a bit on the oranges, but in the end it pretty much balances out. It simplified doing business with me for my clients; to me that's worth a lot!

As *simplification* gets hot, the organizations that will thrive are those that have the entire organization focused on simplifying every component element of the way it interfaces with the outside world. They'll typically take advantage of opportunities to *simplify* internal interactions, procedures, and processes as well.

Community Catalysts Conquer

The *community catalysts conquer* trend is about businesses taking the initiative to create a broader sense of community among their customers and where appropriate, other stakeholders.

Being the 'supplier of choice' may be part of your organization's mission statement. Becoming a *community catalyst* is getting beyond being simply the 'supplier of choice'. Doing things that foster a relationship, beyond just a point of purchase for products or services, is what leading edge organizations across industry lines are doing right now.

A large scale version of this concept in action is user groups facilitated by software and technology companies. When these groups began to form, many of these suppliers fought against them, or were, at the very least, reluctant to be involved. They worried that they would become forums for their customers to gang up on them, and create no end of problems.

What happened is that they became a tremendous source of helpful suggestions and good ideas. They also became mechanisms for their customers to solve problems for each other. Now an entrenched part of the entire technology sector, the broader concept can be applied in almost every business setting.

A clothing and accessories retailer in Singapore, 77th Street, focuses solely on the teenage market. In every city, there is a store that is the 'cool' place for this crowd at any given moment in time. Very few maintain that position for very long. CEO Elim Chew has kept 77th Street in this position in Singapore for over 20 years.

The website for 77th Street has an 'events' section; 'My Voice' provides a bulletin board and chat facility. In Singapore, 77th Street is more than a store; it's a community. (Elim Chew's latest initiative is the 77th Street Plaza Shopping Mall in Beijing, which opened averaging over 300,000 shoppers per day!)

In Johannesburg, Lifestyle Garden Center has become an icon, garnering a hugely disproportionate share of the market for plants and landscaping supplies. They run several different clubs onsite for specific gardening interest groups, and host a wide variety of events that appeal to those involved or interested in gardening. There is something going on there all the time.

Check the webpage for your local Apple store. There is a seminar or tutorial going on every day. They run programs to teach kids how to make movies, and other cool stuff, and sponsor contests for local schools.

In 2008, Nike sponsored a million-person run; a series of short runs and marathons, happening in cities all over the world on the same day. The event raised money for charity. Nike's website made it easy to sign up, and invite friends to join the experience.

More than just the traditional 'sponsoring an event', these businesses are taking the initiative to create a sense of community. People meet others with at least one thing in common, and then move a bit beyond the "a place where I buy stuff" relationship with the retailer. These businesses are using their brands and marketing power to be a *catalyst* for something else.

In Holland, the Ikea store organized a furniture swap at its Amsterdam store. Ikea's website lets people draw the rooms in their houses, place their furniture in them, and then move the pieces around. After rearranging things, and having pieces left over, they were invited to bring them to the store and trade them for things others had brought. (They did not need to be Ikea items). The idea was a giant, upscale yard sale, but for free. Ikea added about $15,000 worth of merchandise to the mix. It's a pretty safe bet that a group of people, in the midst of redecorating, standing in an Ikea store, interacting with other Ikea customers, is good for sales! More than that, it's an event that brought customers together and showcased Ikea's willingness to be helpful – clever way for a furniture store to capture the concept.

KLM Airlines has a mechanism to connect its golfing passengers. If you are taking your golf clubs on a trip to China, then with your permission, they connect you with other passengers also taking their clubs on the same flight.

At the extreme end of the *community catalysts* continuum is the Ebbsfleet United Football Club in England. This unique initiative allowed individuals to band together to create a new football club (What North Americans call a soccer team).

Via the web, people were invited to chip in approximately $50 to a pool of money to be held in trust. If they collected enough money, they'd buy a team. (They needed millions.) Everyone who contributed would own a small piece. If not, they'd return the money.

Well, they did it, and as this book goes to press, they are sorting out how the management will be put in place and players chosen. I expect they've been a *catalyst* for what will become a most passionate *community!*

This community phenomenon is obvious in the explosion of sites like YouTube, Facebook, and hundreds of others. Originally for college students, many of us see these sites as appealing to the 20-something crowd. Today, over half the Facebook users are 35 years old or older, and the fastest growing demographic on the site in the first half of 2009 was women over 55.

These 'community happenings' are different from the traditional, more social 'client appreciation' type events. In the *Age of Hollywood Days & Cyber Knights*, everyone's calendar is jammed. Teach me something of interest, present a speaker I won't see elsewhere, offer me an experience I cannot otherwise have, and I'll make time. Those doing this well are thriving and setting good foundations for future success.

The 'corporate alumni' initiatives we talked about earlier are another example of this same concept in action.

Someone has to design, plan, execute, monitor, and follow up all these kinds of efforts. As more and more businesses begin to understand the power of becoming a *community catalyst*, the demand for those who can help them do it successfully will grow.

What is your organization doing to be a *community catalyst*? How can *you* help?

More Trends to Watch

Here's a short summary of several other trends that should also be on your radar screen:

- **Insourcing Innovation**

More and more organizations are working to defeat the 'not invented here' syndrome. In today's marketplace, the speed necessary to keep up with the introduction of new products and services is almost impossible to achieve, solely with internal resources. Smart organizations are recognizing that multiple constituencies have the capacity to contribute to their innovation process.

The transition Proctor & Gamble has made over the last few years illustrates this concept. Proctor & Gamble had thousands of people in its internal Research & Development departments, justifiably proud of a very lengthy track record of delivering innovative products. (Some wags claim that it was Proctor & Gamble that invented 'not invented here'!)

Recently they changed their focus from 'research and develop' to 'connect and develop'. By proactively finding others to contribute ideas and expertise to their own R & D efforts, they built relationships to expand their creative base.

The results in both cost and speed have been stunning. The first fruit of this new approach was the introduction of *Swiffer*. This has certainly been a monstrously successful line of products.

So, *insourcing innovation* is about finding the answers to these questions:
> Who else can we involve?
> What other ways can we spread our tentacles into broader idea pools?
> How do we devise structure and mechanisms to pull external creative thinking and expertise into our internal innovation initiatives?

■ The Value is in The Analysis

Any organization that differentiates itself from other organizations by providing analysis of specific, useful information is of great value to its customer base.

The days of customers perceiving value in getting information, by itself, are gone. The marketplace has more data than it can possibly need; what is necessary is specific, useful information. Almost every organization knows more about some particular segment of its customer's operation than the customer can possibly know. The organization knows industry trends, benchmarks, comparatives, etc. The value it uniquely provides is in analyzing the information available and making it specifically useful to its customer.

Information may still be power in some arenas, but in the marketplace, it is the *analysis* of information that provides value.

Sometimes this is understanding how to best use individual capabilities to allow others to access or compile information more simply than by doing it all themselves.

The website for Bugaboo strollers provides its visitors with the ability to look up dozens of cities and find places of interest that are easily accessible when pushing a stroller.

Courier companies save millions of calls to their call centers by making their tracking software available to their customers.

Sometimes it is determining what other kind of information you can provide that will be of specific information to your customers. For example, when the Starwood Hotel chain sends an email confirmation, they attach a weather forecast for the days around the planned visit.

In a more complex form, this is about asking questions – What else do we know how to do that is of value? What other information can we crunch and uniquely provide that is valuable to our customers? At other times it is simply analyzing what other information will be particularly useful to customers, while saving them the time and frustration of finding it on their own.

The information is all out there. The value is in thinking through how to analyze it and present it to our customers.

■ "Hold Hands and Stay Together"

This trend is all about networks and alliances. The expression comes from a wonderful little book written several years ago, *All I Really Need to Know I Learned in Kindergarten* by Robert Fulghum. One of the pieces of advice in that book is, "Hold hands and stay together."

All organizations have partnerships and strategic alliances. Most are the obvious connections in their specific areas of business. For example, if you are an insurance company, you have relationships with reinsurance companies and insurance brokers.

This trend encourages organizations to think creatively – with what other organizations may they be able to connect, in some fashion, to provide better value for their clients. It's a great thing to form trusted relationships with clients. What we're watching now are more and more organizations thinking creatively about how they can form relationships with others who already have a trusted relationship, with the customer base they want to reach.

Shortly after Hurricane Katrina, Home Depot formed a relationship with MTV, creating the 'Alternate Spring Break', bringing students to New Orleans to help with rebuilding efforts.

This is happening in a variety of industries and in organizations of all sizes. In the land of the giants, Nike has hooked up with Apple to connect a Nano iPod via Bluetooth to Nike running shoes, allowing runners to record the statistics of their runs. The information can be uploaded to the Nike website where fitness fans can track, on a daily basis, how far they went, how many steps they took, how many calories they burned, etc. There is also a connection to the iTunes site, which has a variety of music for specific exercise activities – stamina, strength, speed, etc.

A good way to start the creative thought processes to capture this trend is to ask. Who has our client before we do? Whose client do we have before they do?

I tell executives to answer this question: Who *else* should you be having lunch with? The exploratory conversations need to focus on what each party can bring to the table, helping both organizations better serve an identified, common client base.

The organizations that are doing well are those that have a wide variety of these creative relationships and alliances, helping them strengthen the bonds they have with existing customers, while moving more quickly to create relationships in new markets or with new client segments.

"Hold hands and stay together" is still pretty good advice.

■ Risk Reduction Rules

The focus here is how to *reduce the risk* factor for our customers.

The world today is increasingly virtual, and more of what we are paying for is intangible. Everyone is more conscious of the inherent risk in discovering that what is promised is often not what is delivered.

There have always been 'money-back-guarantees'. However, the bar for guarantees is continually being raised.

Around the beginning of 2009, as economic turmoil was enveloping the United States, the Hyundai car manufacturer introduced a program saying that if you bought a new car from them and then lost your job, they would take the car back, no strings attached. Very quickly, others followed suit with similar initiatives. Hyundai, however, was there first, and saw a 14% jump in sales when virtually every other car manufacturer was seeing double-digit declines.

Charles Tyrwhitt is a men's shirt retailer in England. On its website, for several years, the guarantee policy has said, "If any shirt fails to meet with your approval you can return it within three months of purchase, washed or unwashed, for an exchange or a full and immediate refund."

Lots of factors contribute to businesses success. In the 20 years since it started Charles Tyrwhitt has become the largest shirt retailer in the UK. This happened against many competitors, some of whom had more than a century's head start in the shirt retailing business.

Organizations looking for a 'leg up' in the marketplace are examining their own guarantee / warranty policies. Are they complex, mealy-mouth, 'repair or replace at our sole discretion' statements, that appear to be designed to make sure that no monies ever need to be returned; or are they simple, straightforward expressions of confidence, prominently displayed and designed to reduce the risk factor for people considering doing business with that specific organization?

■ Recruiting Goes Full Time

I've left this trend to last, because in 2009, this topic may seem like the least obvious trend to which organizations should be devoting energy. Yet, the hunt for talent never stops.

In a world where innovation, talent, networks, and reputations are huge factors in success, the ability to attract top-notch talent is critical. Smart organizations make recruiting a key, strategic priority and continue to explore, in depth, a wide variety of initiatives available for becoming a prominent 'employer of choice' in their marketplace.

The headlines across the first half of 2009, say, "This economy is an unprecedented economic calamity." Over the last 150 years the free market economies have spent somewhere between 7% and 12% of their time in some type of dramatic, economic turbulence.

As each of those situations ended, so this will end. As it ends, there will once again be a great battle for talent. The organizations that will thrive are those who are investing some portion of their time and energy NOW determining how to win that battle.

There are many component factors that help transform any business into an effective recruiting machine. Here's one that everyone controls at an individual level – it answers this question: How do we talk about our company in front of strangers?

Here's how I see the individual's role in this big picture. Our career opportunities and the atmosphere of our day-to-day working lives are better when we are part of an organization that is successful.

Organizations succeed, in large part because of what outsiders think of them. It seems to me, if organizations are better off when outsiders think well of them, it makes sense for those inside these organizations to be conscious of how they talk about each other and their organizations in front of others.

I am constantly amazed and appalled at the conversations I innocently overhear about organizations from their own people. I hear them in elevators, restaurants, and waiting lines of every sort. I hear people identifying and talking about the organizations they work for in the most unflattering terms.

No organization is perfect. There are always things that need to be changed or that some wish they could change about their organization. There is a time and a place for airing grievances about the organization. There is a time and a place for letting off steam. Any public environment is NOT one of those places!

In an airport recently, I listened to a 'road warrior' on a cell phone. I couldn't help but listen, as everyone else in the waiting area at Gate B29 was also party to this conversation, whether they wanted to be or not. While on his cell phone, this very vocal 'road warrior' was discussing the details of a proposal he and some of his colleagues were submitting.

Both the windbreaker he was wearing and his luggage clearly identified his employer. It was a classic 'What were you thinking?' kind of moment; he obviously had no idea who any of the dozens of other people within earshot of this conversation were.

It's easy to point a finger at one individual in one situation. But confidentiality issues aside, I see this kind of thing often enough to know that there are lots of folks, who need to be reminded that cumulatively, how we talk about our organization in public has an influence on how our organization is perceived by others.

All of us have a role to play in helping our organizations become an 'employer of choice' to win the coming recruiting battles.

"And in Summary..."

Well, here we are at the end of our tour of the evolving world of work, for administrative professionals, and some of the major trends impacting all of our organizations.

We've talked about:

- ✓ The Age of Hollywood Days & Cyber Knights.
- ✓ 'Hollyworking'
- ✓ Planning & Pursuing the Future You Want
- ✓ 'Gumption'
- ✓ Activity vs. Results
- ✓ Personality *is* the Brand
- ✓ Micro-marketing
- ✓ The Next Service Revolution: Customer Intelligence
- ✓ Simplification Gets Hot!
- ✓ Community Catalysts Conquer

And we touched on:

- Insourcing Innovation
- The Value is in the Analysis
- "Hold Hands and Stay Together"
- Risk Reduction Rules
- Recruiting Goes Full Time

We've covered a lot of ground in a short space, both for you and for your organization.

So, what's next for you?

You have a very fundamental choice: you can either adapt what you've read to fit your model of the world, OR, you can adapt your model of the world in light of this information.

I believe that what is true for organizations is also true for individuals:
The market shall sit in judgment between the quick and the dead.
The rich don't bury the poor, the creative bury the stagnant.
The smart don't beat the dumb, the flexible beat the rigid.
The strong don't crush the weak, the agile outperform the habitual.

Here's the happy news if you are planning to act on the information and ideas in this book – most people won't.

That perhaps sounds harsh. But it's true.

Look around your office. Many are ambitious, perhaps. But how many are prepared to understand what's going on around them, take a good look at themselves, make a plan, and then do the work to act on it? How many are really career-minded professionals?

The broadly accurate answer – Not many.

Only you know the answer to the important question: Are you one of them?

You know the old expression: "When all is said and done, there's usually a lot more said than done." Many will intend; few will do.

This is just human nature. It's normal. You don't have to be. You can be one of the small percentage that decides to take charge of your future, and take action.

You can do this. It's about the disciplined execution of good ideas.

If this was an enjoyable read, with some interesting information, and useful ideas, then we are both happy you've read the book.

Now go start building the future you want for yourself.

Today.

Warren's Coordinates

To check Warren's availability for speaking engagements, drop a line to Sarah@FutureOfWork.com

To schedule a Strategic Planning program for your organization, or to enquire about the *Think, Prioritise, Execute* process for the Executive teams of small and mid-sized enterprises, please connect with Patti@WEvans.com

Warren's direct e-mail is Warren@WEvans.com

Or should the mood strike, do feel free to pick up the phone. Toronto is the same time zone as New York City.

North America: 800 – 364 – 3205
Sydney: 02 – 8003 – 4746
London   02071 – 938 – 263
Direct: +1 – 905 – 858 - 0000
Skype: Warren-Evans

www.WEvans.com